ADHD Workbook for Adults

Skills to Improve Concentration, Organization, Stress Management in Difficult Situations: Including Work, School, and Personal Relationships

Gerald Paul Clifford

© Copyright 2020 by Gerald Paul Clifford. All right reserved.

The work contained herein has been produced with the intent to provide relevant knowledge and information on the topic on the topic described in the title for entertainment purposes only. While the author has gone to every extent to furnish up to date and true information, no claims can be made as to its accuracy or validity as the author has made no claims to be an expert on this topic. Notwithstanding, the reader is asked to do their own research and consult any subject matter experts they deem necessary to ensure the quality and accuracy of the material presented herein.

This statement is legally binding as deemed by the Committee of Publishers Association and the American Bar Association for the territory of the United States. Other jurisdictions may apply their own legal statutes. Any reproduction, transmission, or copying of this material contained in this work without the express written consent of the copyright holder shall be deemed as a copyright violation as per the current legislation in force on the date of publishing and the subsequent time thereafter. All additional works derived from this material may be claimed by the holder of this copyright.

The data, depictions, events, descriptions, and all other information forthwith are considered to be true, fair, and accurate unless the work is expressly described as a work of fiction. Regardless of the nature of this work, the Publisher is exempt from any responsibility of actions taken by the reader in conjunction with this work. The Publisher acknowledges that the reader acts of their own accord and releases the author and Publisher of any responsibility for the observance of tips, advice, counsel, strategies, and techniques that may be offered in this volume.

Table of Contents

Introduction 7
Chapter 1: Understanding ADHD 11

What Is ADHD? 11
Why Does ADHD Happen? 12
Types of ADHD 14
What Is Adult ADHD? 15
ADHD Diagnosis in Adults 17
What Challenges Are Faced By Adults Who Have ADHD? 20

Chapter 2: Characteristics of ADHD 26

Distractibility and Difficulty to Concentrate 26
Impulsivity 28
Hyperactivity 29
Exaggerated Emotions 30
Gender and ADHD 33

Chapter 3: Making Time for Mindfulness and Exercise 37

Is Mindfulness Effective for ADHD? 38
Exercise and ADHD 43
Common Types of Exercises That Help Alleviate the Symptoms of ADHD 46

Chapter 4: How Can You Minimize the Triggers? 51

Some Common Triggers to be Aware of 51

Food Additives 51
Mineral Deficiencies 52
Stress 53
Poor Sleep 54
Technology 55

Tips for Minimizing Triggers 56

Maintain a Balanced Diet 56
Exercise Regularly 57
Work On Your Time Management Skills 57
Spend Time Outdoors 59
Get Enough Sleep 59

Chapter 5: Behavioral Therapy for ADHD ... 62

How Does Behavioral Therapy Work? 62
CBT for Adults 64

What Is CBT? 64
How Does CBT Help ADHD Adults? 67

What Is DBT? 74

Chapter 6: A Step-by-Step Guide to Become More Productive With ADHD 75

Step 1 - Don't Try Multitasking 75
Step 2 - Be Realistic 78
Step 3 – Stop Trying to be Perfect 79
Step 4 – Prep Your Environment 81
Step 5 – Time Your Tasks 84
Step 6 – Do the Fun Stuff First 85
Step 7 – Use Visual Reminders 86

Chapter 7: Treating ADHD With Medication 88

Stimulant Medications 90
Non-Stimulant Medications 96
When Should I Take Medications?........................ 99

Chapter 8: Dealing With ADHD Shame 104

What Is Shame? 104
Consequences of Shame 108
How to Silence the Haters? 110
How to Heal Shame? 113
Practice Self-Love 115

Chapter 9: ADHD and Relationships 121

What Is the Impact of ADHD on Relationships? . 121
Tips for a Healthier Relationship 125

Conclusion 128
Resources 133

Introduction

Congratulations on purchasing *ADHD Workbook for Adults,* and thank you for doing so.

In this book, you will find every detail that you need to know about ADHD and then learn the techniques with the help of which you can make your life easier. There are strategies that will help you identify ADHD in a person. Finding out that you have ADHD is one of the first steps towards recovering from the problem. The earlier you identify the disorder, the sooner you will get the treatment, and the faster you will be able to bring your life back on track.

Some of the most common symptoms of ADHD include disorganization, impulsivity, distractibility, and so on, and you are going to learn about all of these symptoms in detail in this book. One of the most common results of having ADHD is that both your personal and professional life is severely hampered. In the case of adults, they often cruise along with life, and eventually, they arrive at a stage when everything seems to be going wrong and falling apart. That is when they are diagnosed with ADHD.

Most people don't understand how frustrating ADHD can be. It is not only contradictory but also confusing. When people have to spend their day-to-day lives with this condition, it easily gets overwhelming. When you go to a specialist for diagnosis, they will ask you a lot of questions, and they will also provide you with a checklist of symptoms that you can go through. Medication alone is never enough to help you cope with the symptoms. You always need more, and by more, I mean that you need to take the help of therapy.

Most of us think that ADHD means a kid who is bouncing on the couch and running wildly around the house. But is that the only type of ADHD that you need to be aware of? No, because ADHD can happen to adults too, and that is not how it looks. In fact, there are several adults with ADHD who are not hyperactive, but they have other symptoms. Some people believe that ADHD is one of the most over-diagnosed conditions, but whether that is true or not, you have to understand that the implications on the life of the person are immense. They cannot keep up with their personal relationships, and they forget about stuff very easily. They make impulsive decisions and might go on a shopping spree all of a sudden just because they feel like it, or they might shift between jobs every month. But more often than not, these people are not particularly happy about the decisions they are taking and so, they regret it later. Their patterns and actions are mostly very self-destructive, and they easily fall into the clutches of depression ad addiction. The effort and struggle that has to be given by an ADHD individual are way more than anyone else who is doing the same thing.

We are not only going to break several myths surrounding ADHD, but we are also going to learn about several tactics that can help you cope with your symptoms and lead a more organized life. I know that maintaining a healthy routine can be your biggest nightmare when you have ADHD but trust me, with the proven strategies mentioned here, you are going to learn a lot of self-control and make a lot of improvement with routines.

I am sure that your doctor is going to suggest some medications for this, but that will not be enough. So, in order to get your priorities straight and getting things organized, you will need the help of a therapist. Whenever it comes to making a choice that needs to be made after considerable thought, it's best if you take a time out and then negotiate. If there are any negative feelings inside you, then they have to be removed by someone you trust in order to be able to make your recovery faster. You need this help, even more, when you think that you have not been able to keep up with the expectations of others.

Another thing to keep in mind is that just because someone is energetic and always enthusiastic about stuff, you cannot predict them to have ADHD. You will always find people who are not the quiet type, and they cannot seem to focus their mind on any one thing. So, they keep changing their focus from time to time. But that doesn't make them a patient of ADHD. In this book, you will learn many such facts about ADHD that are not that well-known among people, and that is what creates so much confusion. I am sure that all of you must have come across family members and friends who were all ready to give you advice on what ADHD is and how it can be cured. But most of them are unknown to what ADHD really is. So, before taking any advice from others, I suggest you read this book and consult a specialist for proper diagnosis.

I would also like to give you a small piece of advice here – don't try to finish this book in a rush. I know that most of you would want to finish it in a week. I know that you are also going to feel a sense of accomplishment once you finish this book, but if you want to truly get something out of this, then you need to learn the strategies by heart. And for that, you need to give this some time. It would help if you blocked time in your calendar with the intention of actually doing some work on your problem while reading this book. You have to remind yourself why you are doing this – it is because you want to. If you want change – a change that is going to stay – then you also need to put in the effort. Remind yourself that you deserve, and that is why you have undertaken this journey. And soon, you will see that with these skills under your belt, navigating through life has become so much easier.

There is no end to the number of books on this subject that you will get in the market, but I am thankful that you chose this one. I have tried my best to explain every detail in the most concise manner possible, and so I hope you enjoy it!

Chapter 1: Understanding ADHD

ADHD is a very common disorder. More than 10 million cases of ADHD are recorded in India per year. Here we will discuss the disorder in detail about the cause of this disorder, types, diagnosis, challenges faced by people suffering from this disorder, etc.

What Is ADHD?

The full form of this acronym is Attention-Deficit Hyperactivity Disorder. Out of all the people in the U.S, approximately 4.4% of the adult population is affected by this disorder which is mainly neurological in origin. It is more likely to occur to men than to women. 5.4 percent of men are diagnosed with ADHD, whereas 3.2 percent of women are diagnosed with ADHD. It is a disorder that causes a deficiency of attention and causes heightened levels of impulsive and hyperactive behaviors. Patients who have ADHD have low persistence, face difficulty in focusing on a particular thing, and are disorganized. They are always restless and find extreme difficulty in being calm. They often tend to make impulsive decisions because of the hyperactivity, which may end up proving to be harmful to them.

Earlier, ADHD was considered to be just a childhood condition, but now it is accepted to be an adulthood condition as well. The rates of persistence of ADHD vary from 6 percent to 30 percent. The persistence rates can be even higher, too.

Studies have shown that in the last decade, there is a hike in the rate of ADHD diagnosis among adults in the U.S. (Winston Chung, 2019)

Why Does ADHD Happen?

Though the exact causes of ADHD are still unknown, there are certain factors that definitely play a part in the development of this disorder. Let us see some of those factors.

- *Hereditary:* ADHD can be inherited. If your parent suffers from this disorder, you have a risk of inheriting the same. Certain genetic characteristics pass down through the generation. You have a more than 50 percent chance of developing this disorder if your parent has it, and you have more than 30 percent chance of developing this disorder if your older sibling has it. However, the inheritance of ADHD is way more complex, so it is not just because of a single genetic fault.

- *Pregnancy Problems:* ADHD may also develop from certain pregnancy-related problems. A child who is born premature, or is born slightly underweight, has a higher risk of developing this disorder. A child whose mother has had difficult pregnancies earlier is also prone to develop this disorder. The frontal lobe of your brain is responsible for controlling emotions and impulses. So, children having head injuries in this region are at a greater risk of developing this disorder. Pregnant women who drink alcohol or smoke are at a higher risk of giving birth to a child having ADHD. Getting exposed to pesticides, PCBs, or leads, while pregnancy may also increase the chance of the baby developing ADHD.

- *Brain Functions:* After birth, if a child develops some infectious disorder that may affect the brain tissues, like encephalitis or meningitis, then that may affect the working ways of sending signals. This may also induce symptoms of ADHD. Sugar and certain food additives are often considered to induce ADHD. However, researches show that ADHD has got nothing to do with dietary factors.

Chemicals present in the brain, also known as neurotransmitters, work differently in adults and children having ADHD. Even the working ways of the nerve pathways tend to differ. Certain areas of the brain of children having ADHD are smaller or less active than those children who don't have this disorder. The neurotransmitter dopamine also plays a significant role. It is linked to learning, attention, mood, sleep, and movement.

Researches have shown differences in brain activities in people with ADHD and without ADHD. The exact significance is still not clear.

- *Other Factors:* Few groups of people are believed to be at a higher risk of developing ADHD like people who were born premature, i.e., before the thirty-seventh week of pregnancy. People with epilepsy are also prone to develop ADHD. People with brain damage also tend to develop ADHD. This damage can occur either in the mother's womb or can also occur because of a serious injury in the head later in life.

Types of ADHD

ADHD is characterized by hyperactivity, impulsivity, and inattention. Most of the people who don't have ADHD also experience a certain degree of impulsive or inattentive behavior, but people with ADHD experience severe hyperactivity-impulsiveness and inattentiveness. There are three types of ADHD, and each type of ADHD is linked to one or more characteristics. They are as follows:

- *Predominantly Inattentive ADHD*: People suffering from this type of ADHD mostly have symptoms of inattention. Their impulsive nature or hyperactivity is not as much as their inattentiveness. Although, at times, it is possible that they have to struggle with hyperactivity or impulse control, but they are not the main characteristics of predominantly inattentive ADHD. This type of ADHD is more common in girls than in boys.

- *Predominantly Hyperactive-Impulsive ADHD:* People who have predominantly hyperactive-impulsive ADHD have symptoms of impulsivity and hyperactivity more than the symptoms of inattention. Patients having predominantly hyperactive-impulsive ADHD may also be inattentive at times, but that is certainly not the main characteristic of this disorder. Children suffering from this disorder can cause a lot of disturbance in their school's classroom. They make learning way more difficult for other students as well as themselves.

- *Combination ADHD:* If a person has combination ADHD, then it means their symptoms don't exactly fall under hyperactive-impulsive behavior or inattention. Instead, they experience a combination of symptoms of both categories.

What Is Adult ADHD?

Being an adult, balancing everything in your life can be really hectic. If you see that you are constantly forgetful, disorganized, clumsy, late, and always struggling to meet your responsibilities, then it is possible that you have ADHD. ADHD, in adults, can cause a lot of hindrance in both their personal and professional life. If you were diagnosed with ADHD at childhood, then it is possible that you carry those symptoms with you into your adulthood as well. It is also possible that you get diagnosed with ADHD in your adulthood, but while you were a child, you were never diagnosed with ADHD. It is possible for ADHD to remain undiagnosed in childhood. In earlier days, not many people were aware of it. Children having the symptoms of ADHD were mostly termed as troublemakers, slackers, dreamers, etc. in the earlier days, which is why chances of ADHD being undiagnosed were very much high at that time.

When you were a child, you may have been able to compensate for those symptoms of ADHD. But when you grow up, it is not that easy to run away from your responsibilities. When you are a grown-up individual, you are expected to run a household, raise a family, pursue a lucrative career, and many more. These responsibilities demand concentration, calmness, and focus, which become very difficult for an ADHD patient to maintain. Even normal people find it difficult to meet up to all these responsibilities. So, for people with ADHD, this is just straight away impossible. The only good thing about this disorder is that it is treatable. With the help of a little creativity, support, and education, you can be able to overcome the symptoms of ADHD. You can even turn some of your biggest weaknesses into your strengths. Being an adult, it is totally possible for you to fight against this disorder and succeed.

The symptoms of this disorder are mostly noticed at a young age. The symptoms become more clear and evident when the child's circumstances happen to change. For example, when they start to go to school, they show clear symptoms of ADHD. Most of the cases are diagnosed when the children are mostly between 6 to 12 years of age. ADHD symptoms generally improve with age, but there are many people who were diagnosed with ADHD in childhood and still continue to face problems when they are adults. Inattentiveness and restlessness do not always mean that you have ADHD, but it's a possibility. So, you should never ignore these things and should get a proper diagnosis.

ADHD Diagnosis in Adults

ADHD diagnosis in adults is way more difficult than that in kids. The main reason is the presence of varied opinions of whether the symptoms list used to diagnose ADHD in children should also be implied while diagnosing ADHD in adults or not. In some situations, an adult exhibiting five or more symptoms of impulsiveness and hyperactivity, or five or more of inattentiveness symptoms, may be diagnosed with ADHD, as listed in the children's ADHD diagnostic criteria. The specialist must ask you questions about the present symptoms. According to the current diagnostic guideline, ADHD in adults can't be confirmed if the symptoms were not present since childhood. In case you find difficulties in remembering the problems you faced as a child, the clinician may ask your parents, closed ones, or even check your old school records to search for any abnormality that you possessed as a child. In order to get diagnosed with ADHD, an adult must have certain effects on different areas of life. If the adult faces problems in difficulty in maintaining relationships with their partner and family, or if he faces difficulty in keeping and making friends, or if he tends to drive his car very roughly, then he is likely to have ADHD. If your problems are recent and not repetitive and old, then you are not going to get diagnosed with ADHD.

Most of the criteria that are used for diagnosing ADHD in adults are mainly focused on the identification of symptoms in children and teens. So, there are higher chances of misdiagnosis in adults. In order to perform a proper diagnosis of ADHD patients, the physicians must know the nuances of ADHD and must also be aware of the overlapping conditions developed in adulthood. Earlier doctors believed that ADHD is a disorder that only children could have, but with time, it is clearly evident that a lot of adults are facing the symptoms of ADHD later in life and are seeking an evaluation in their adulthood. So, the understanding of ADHD diagnosis has improved quite a lot in the last few decades. Most people try to compensate for the symptoms of ADHD in their own way. These undiagnosed ADHD patients often try to fight inattentiveness, impulsiveness, and hyperactivity because they are good problem solvers, creative, and bright. But when they are overwhelmed with continuous increasing challenges and responsibilities, that is when reality kicks in, and they seek medical help. According to a certified adult psychiatrist, the average age of ADHD diagnosis is 39 in his practice.

There is a symptom guide to diagnose ADHD in children, but there is no such guide or manual to diagnose ADHD in adults. The only way of successful diagnosis of ADHD in adults is to run a thorough clinical interview to obtain a detailed medical history. It is imperative that the patient goes to a clinician who is particularly specialized in ADHD. This is to make sure that the clinician will take out time to gather all the required information from you in order to diagnose ADHD in adulthood. The clinical interview may also incorporate neurophysiological testing in order to obtain greater insight into the subject's weaknesses and strengths. This will help to identify any comorbid or co-existing conditions.

Most of the physicians miss out on the differential diagnosis. ADHD symptoms often are the results of different mental health issues like a mood disorder or anxiety. The clinician must have a thorough understanding of the comorbid conditions. The emotional sensitivity resulting from ADHD may also appear as mere anxiety or a mood disorder. It is the duty of the clinician to understand how these symptoms can mimic each other and at what point they differ; otherwise, you will just end up wasting energy, time, and money. A clinician who is trained in just one of these conditions may end up making the wrong diagnosis. So, the clinician must have proper knowledge of ADHD and everything associated with it in order to perform a successful diagnosis of his or her patients. In order to find a good clinician, it is advised that you go to a directory who will guide you about whom you should pursue. Physicians who have no experience of performing mental health diagnoses must refer their patients to a psychologist or psychiatrist having relevant experience of diagnosing ADHD patients.

What Challenges Are Faced By Adults Who Have ADHD?

Adult ADHD has a massive impact on one's life. If it remains ineffectively treated, untreated, or undiagnosed, it can have adverse effects on the quality of life led by a person and psychological well-being.

- *Career Challenges:* ADHD symptoms like forgetfulness, procrastination, poor concentration, and poor time management may make maintaining a healthy life at the workplace and school very much difficult. Many studies have shown that people having ADHD suffers tremendously in their school life and workplace (Aparajita B. Kuriyan, 2012). Studies have shown that people suffering from

ADHD who did not receive proper treatment at childhood faces extreme difficulty in maintaining and gaining employment compared to other people (Anne Halmøy, 2009). They feel a constant sense of underachievement and faces difficulty in following corporate rules, following a 9 to 5 routine, and maintaining deadlines. Another big problem is finances. People having ADHD are prone to have difficulties in financial management, as well. They struggle with due debt, late fees, lost paperwork, unpaid bills, etc. because of impulsive spending.

- *Relationship Problems:* Symptoms of ADHD like impulsivity, inefficiency to follow tasks, low frustration tolerance, and poor listening skills tend to have a detrimental impact on social connections, familial relationships, friendships, and romantic relationships (Ylva Ginsberg, 2014). You may feel tired because of the constant nagging of your loved ones for you to put yourself together. People close to you may feel hurt because of your insensitivity and irresponsibility. The effects of ADHD may lead to loss of confidence, disappointment, hopelessness, frustration, and embarrassment. You can get a feeling as if you can never get a hold of your life and live up to your fullest potential, leaving you with low self-esteem. You tend to hurt your loved one's expectations, ending up hurting them as well as yourself for not being able to meet their expectations.

- *Criminal Tendencies:* Certain researches have linked adult ADHD to rule-breaking, criminality, and other safety and legal issues, which includes a heightened chance of getting into car accidents as compared to other people without ADHD (Zheng Chang, 2017). Certain studies also show that individuals exhibiting ADHD symptoms are more likely to get engaged in various criminal activities compared to other people. A recent study showed that 26 percent of prisoners have adult ADHD (Stéphanie Baggio, 2018).

It is seen that men who had childhood ADHD are 2 to 3 times more likely to be incarcerated, convicted, or arrested in their adulthood compared to those who don't have ADHD. The impulsivity that lies within the people suffering from ADHD impairs their ability to control emotions, behavior, and thoughts. Their self-regulating capability is also damaged. A study showed that there is a link between criminal behavior and impaired self-control (Alexander T. Vazsonyi, 2017).

Children suffering from ODD (Oppositional Defiant Disorder) portray a very disobedient, hostile, defiant, and negative behavior towards the authorities and parents. They often show resentful, vindictive, and angry behavior. They grow up and gradually tend to incline towards various criminal activities. 25 to 75 percent of people having ADHD also have ODD.

- *Substance Abuse Tendencies:* Substance abuse and adult ADHD are strongly linked. Substance Use Disorder or SUD is very common in patients with ADHD than those who have not been diagnosed with this disorder. In fact, it is two times more likely to happen to ADHD patients. Many adults suffering from ADHD and having a SUD report uses drugs and alcohol to manage ADHD symptoms and self-medicate.

- *Comorbid Disorder:* 60 to 70 percent of people suffering from adult ADHD have a comorbid disorder. According to a study on adult ADHD, about 15 percent of them were found to have a substance abuse disorder diagnosis, 50 percent of them were found to have anxiety disorder diagnosis, and 40 percent of them were diagnosed with a mood disorder (Benjamín Piñeiro-Dieguez, 2016).

- *Health Issues:* ADHD symptoms can also contribute to a wide range of health problems like chronic tension, stress, substance abuse, compulsive eating, etc. People suffering from ADHD often tend to forget to take vital medicines, skip doctor's appointments, ignore medical instructions, neglect vital checkups, and thus are more likely to get themselves into trouble.

If you suffer from ADHD, then that might not be the only health issue you have. ADHD often brings other health issues along with it. Adults suffering from ADHD may have health issues due to alcohol and drugs, sleep problems, depression, etc.

- *Depression:* ADHD is very much likely to make you feel frustrated and sad at times. Clinical depression is very much different than just being sad. It is way more severe and causes the day to day problems in social activities, relationships, school, work, etc. 70 percent of the people who have ADHD get treated for depression at some point in their life.

- *Sleep Problems:* Problems with sleep cycles are very common in people who have ADHD. Even kids with ADHD find it difficult to obtain enough rest. People with ADHD are two to three times more likely to have sleep problems than those who don't have ADHD.

- *Serious Behavioral Problems:* People with ADHD often develop ODD (Oppositional Defiant Disorder). In this, people tend to resentment and anger without any proper reason. They often have a tendency to blame others for their own bad behavior. They purposely annoy people and tend to break the rules and argue with everyone.

Another behavioral disorder noticed in people with ADHD is CD (Conduct Disorder). ODD often turns into CD and becomes more severe. Forty-five percent of teens who have ADHD tend to develop CD later in their life, and 25 percent of children suffering from ADHD also develop CD later in their life. People with CD tend to skip school, steal, destroy properties, and shows extreme aggressive behavior towards animals and people.

Chapter 2: Characteristics of ADHD

In the previous chapter, I already told you about the different types of ADHD that are there. But the symptoms of ADHD fall into two main categories which are –

- Impulsiveness and hyperactivity
- Inattentiveness

There are some people who have symptoms from both categories while there are others who face only one of them. In this chapter, we are going to talk about the characteristics of ADHD in detail. But remember that you are not to use the information mentioned in this chapter for performing self-diagnosis. You can, however, refer to the information in order to figure out for certain whether your problem needs special attention or not. Once you visit a specialist, he/she will be able to diagnose the problem to be ADHD or something else.

Distractibility and Difficulty to Concentrate

Distractibility will, no doubt, be one of the biggest barriers in your path when you are trying to deal with ADHD. But first, let us explore what the term 'distractibility' truly means. It means that you don't have the ability to steer clear of visual distractions or any other unimportant distractions and do the task that you have been assigned. For example, there are several adults with ADHD who simply cannot work when there is the slightest noise in their surroundings – it can be something as simple as someone's footsteps. In short, when people have ADHD, they sort of do not know how to filter out the distractions. So, when there are too many things happening in their surroundings, all of that automatically starts competing for her attention.

When a person with ADHD experiences this feeling of distractibility, they cannot usually frame it in words. This is mainly because they themselves do not understand it that well. People often see them as space cadets or airheads. In fact, when ADHD goes unnoticed or undiagnosed until adulthood, people who struggle with distractibility often think that they are scatterbrained and that it cannot possibly be a part of any disorder. That is why it is so important that you address the problem of distractibility separately in your treatment plan because it is definitely one of the most overwhelming parts of suffering from ADHD.

Another thing to note here is that distractibility is not a symptom that is present at all times in the patient. For example, if a person is being attended to individually, he/she might remain focused and not be distracted.

Impulsivity

Impulsivity is one of those symptoms of ADHD that people often ignore. Being impulsive doesn't only mean that the person has zero sense of self-discipline or is rude. There is much more to it than just that. Impulsiveness comes from changes in the brain's signaling system, which is impacted in a person with ADHD. So, a person takes random actions without thinking it through. They completely overlook the consequences that their actions are going to have. They simply act on a whim. So, an adult with ADHD might answer people rudely all of a sudden or scream because they are angry.

The different parts of the brain are responsible for different activities. Similarly, it is your thalamus that is responsible for impulse control. Its function is very similar to that of a gate because it is the thalamus that decides which signals it is going to stop and which it is going to allow. So, if a signal comes along that is a red flag, the frontal cortex is made known of it by the thalamus with the help of the limbic-hippocampal connections. The frontal cortex of the brain is the region that is responsible for solving problems and handling your expression of different emotions. But when someone has ADHD, the gate of the thalamus does not function the way it normally should. So, they face difficulty in holding back their words even when they know that what they are going to say might hurt someone badly. This is also why ADHD adults go on a shopping spree from time to time because they cannot put a rein on their money-spending impulses.

It is because of impulsiveness that people act at the spur of the moment. You can also say that these people do not have a good sense of judgment and very poor planning skills. Gradually, they become disorganized and disorderly. The symptom of distractibility, along with impulsiveness, is what makes these people so untidy with cluttered work desks, unpaid bills, untucked shirts, missed deadlines, and careless writing style. Another part of this impulsiveness is antisocial behavior.

Hyperactivity

The characteristics of hyperactivity are more commonly noticed in children than in adults. Even when it comes to adults, you will find that it is men who display this symptom more than women. This symptom refers to the behavior of constant fidgeting and the need to move. Some people have the habit of shuffling their feet or continuously tapping their fingers even while they are in the middle of a conversation. There are different ways in which the symptom of hyperactivity can manifest itself. But you have to keep in mind that when people grow old, hyperactivity is the first symptom that dies down, and so, you cannot identify or diagnose ADHD solely based on hyperactivity. In any case, if someone is suffering from a problem of hyperactivity, they will not be able to sit in a single place for a long time. They will also not prefer doing quiet activities and have a knack towards energetic activities.

Exaggerated Emotions

Emotions are often heightened in adults who have ADHD. The root cause of this characteristic also lies in the brain. Adult ADHD often causes people to get flooded by a certain emotion all of a sudden, even though that emotion was only momentary. This is mainly because of some problems in the working memory. Unfortunately, the system of diagnosis, that is currently followed for ADHD, doesn't factor in exaggerated emotions or emotional challenges. But if we are to follow the research-based evidence, then we'll see, then it is shown that people with ADHD have a hot temper, impatience, a very low tolerance level to frustration, and excitability.

These challenges that we are talking about also find their origin in the human brain. In usual scenarios, anyone who has ADHD won't seem that much affected by someone's feelings or actions and would appear to be completely unaware. But there are times when these emotions become exaggerated because of impairments. Our emotions are relayed through various signals in the brain, and in people with ADHD, these networks do not function the way they should and are somewhat limited.

So, if something is denied to the adult, they often get filled with rage and cannot keep their anger under control even when the issue is not that important. Thus, they end up giving an extreme response to something very insignificant. This phenomenon is also known as flooding because the emotion at that point of time has taken up all the space inside his/her head. It is very similar to a virus attack on your laptop, where the laptop does not function properly because the virus takes up the entire hard disk. So, the person starts focusing on that one single emotion and overlooks everything else. They cannot take in any information that is given to them at that moment. That is why any attempt to regulate or reduce their anger doesn't work out.

Another example of having exaggerated emotions is that people with ADHD are very sensitive to any kind of disapproval. That one salient emotion becomes so superior in their minds that they cannot focus on anything else. So, let us say some coworker has disapproved the patient's idea on a project. Even though the disapproval was done in a very polite manner, the patient might think of it as extreme criticism, and they would right away go into a self-defense mode. Their outburst at that moment would be so huge that anyone would think something grave has happened. Only if the patient had been listening to his/her carefully, they would have been able to understand that it was not a criticism at all.

Adults who have ADHD also face a lot of social anxiety that they keep bottled up inside themselves. They are constantly in this cycle of self-loathing because they feel that they are uncool, unappealing, and not competent enough like everyone around them. This can be really toxic and make life even more difficult for an ADHD patient.

At other times, people with ADHD do understand the emotion, but they are too scared to deal with them. Their tolerance level for those emotions is too low. Whenever something gets serious or is too painful to talk about, it overwhelms them, and so they avoid the topic altogether. This doesn't help in any way to solve the problem. Such behaviors are often noticed when ADHD adults have to be in a social gathering with a bunch of people they don't know or when there are plenty of deadlines knocking on the door.

The ADHD brain is mostly incapable of seeing minor problems and dangerous threats separately, and so, their emotions are always wrong. So, even when a situation does not require them to panic, they start panicking. It is somewhat uncontrollable for them because their brain is wired in such a way. So, an adult having ADHD cannot deal with stressful events, and they cannot behave realistically. When they have to make a decision, thinking rationally seems a big deal to them.

Another example of exaggerated emotions in ADHD adults is that many of them suffer from dysthymia, especially when their ADHD goes untreated for a long duration of time. Dysthymia is characterized by sadness, and it is a mood disorder that often happens over the long term. When the right treatment is not received, adults with ADHD have to deal with a lot of negativity and frustrations in their day-to-day life, and that is what leads to this mood disorder. These people are also seen to have a very poor sense of self-esteem, and their energy levels are always very low.

Every action that we take in our lives is motivated by our emotions. So, when ADHD is either not diagnosed or not treated properly in adults, they often seek immediate gratification, and for this, they pursue only those activities that can give them that. That is why, in the long term, they fail to provide a consistent effort to those tasks whose rewards are going to be realized at a later time. Moreover, there have been several brain imaging studies done on ADHD patients that show that the ADHD brain does not identify satisfaction or pleasure like that of a normal brain, especially for tasks whose rewards are delayed.

Gender and ADHD

In this section, we are going to talk about the characteristics of ADHD with respect to gender. This topic is often overlooked. According to statistics, ADHD is more commonly diagnosed in boys than that in girls, and this disparity has nothing to do with ADHD affecting boys more than girls. This is not an explanation. The more plausible explanation is that the symptoms manifest themselves in different ways in girls and boys. The symptoms in girls are more subtle, and so, people often tend to miss them out.

In research, it has been found that impulsivity and always trying to move and such externalized symptoms are more common in boys (Rucklidge, 2010). On the contrary, in the case of girls, the symptoms are internalized. They have a very poor sense of self-esteem, and they are always inattentive. Another significant difference is that physical aggression is not something that is commonly seen in girls. It is seen in boys, whereas, in girls, it is verbal aggression that is common. But the fact that symptoms in girls are often overlooked means that they are undiagnosed and, thus, left untreated for a very long time. When they move into adulthood and are diagnosed with ADHD, the disorder has already jeopardized their self-esteem to a great extent in all those years. In the case of boys, whenever they feel that their frustration is becoming too much to handle, they take it out externally, but girls, on the other hand, don't do that. They direct their frustration and anger inward and keep blaming themselves for everything. Thus, ADHD in girls leads to some other problems as well, for example, eating disorders and depression.

In 2012, it was found in research that tendency to self-harm and commit suicides is much higher in those girls who are suffering from combined-type ADHD (Stephen P. Hinshaw, 2012). They also mentioned that this tendency stayed despite the fact that symptoms of impulsiveness and hyperactivity had subsided in 40% of them by the time they reached adolescence.

Now that you know that the common symptoms that we talked about at the beginning of this chapter are not usually as prominent in girls, how will you identify that they have ADHD? Well, there are some symptoms that you should keep an eye on, and they are as follows -

- Anxiety
- No or very low sense of self-esteem
- Withdrawn from daily life
- Inability to focus
- Always daydreaming or inattentive
- Poor academic record
- Impairment of intellectuality
- Signs of verbal aggressions in petty situations (name-calling, taunting, teasing, etc.)
- Not listening to others

The most common question that everyone has after learning about this difference in boys and girls is whether the treatment process is different for these genders. Well, the treatment is the same. But whenever someone goes to a doctor, he/she will consider your individual differences because not everyone has the same response, and not everyone has the same behavioral symptoms. So, a particular combination of therapy and medication is fixed for each and every person depending upon their needs.

Chapter 3: Making Time for Mindfulness and Exercise

Attention deficit hyperactivity disorder (ADHD) can show up at different stages of life and in several ways. It happens due to the differences in the brain, which affects important functioning skills like memory, attention, impulsiveness, concentration, and more. For a majority of children and adults suffering from ADHD, maintaining self-regulation and paying attention are two of the persistent daily challenges that they have to face. So, it can be said that a natural remedy for ADHD would be some kind of attention training that helps hone their self-control. It would be incredibly powerful and invaluable.

While the symptoms of ADHD can be managed by therapy and meditation, they are not the only options. According to studies, another good way to improve your focus and calm your mind is through mindfulness meditation. Mindfulness or mindful meditation is a part of several religious traditions like Buddhism. However, it is not necessarily spiritual or religious. It consists of developing a greater awareness of everything that is happening around you every moment by paying close attention to your bodily sensations, feelings, and thoughts. It can also be used as a tool to promote psychological well-being. According to a survey conducted by *ADDitude* magazine in 2017, more than 1/3rd of adults suffering from ADHD use mindfulness, and almost forty percent of them have given it high ratings.

Is Mindfulness Effective for ADHD?

Just like exercises can help strengthen a specific weak muscle in your body, the same thing can also be true for your brain. Mindfulness helps enhance your capacity to control your attention. It allows you to focus on yourself and teaches you how to observe yourself. In addition to that, when you get distracted, mindfulness trains you to bring back your wandering mind to the present moment.

Unlike other treatments for ADHD, practicing mindfulness helps to develop your inner skills. It helps increase your ability to develop different kinds of relationships, to train your attention, and strengthen your ability to self-observe so that you can control your attention. Therefore, it makes you learn how to pay attention to paying attention so that you don't react impulsively and become aware of your emotional state. Meditation thickens the prefrontal cortex of your brain. The prefrontal cortex is the region of your brain that is involved in controlling your impulses, planning, and focusing. It also increases the level of dopamine in your brain, which gets decreased in people who have ADHD. Thus, it is believed that meditation helps people suffering from ADHD.

If you find long durations of sitting meditation to be very overwhelming, here are a few ways to help you get started.

- **Take a Class** – You can try signing up for a meditation class to harness the power of positive peer pressure. Following routines can be hard for people suffering from ADHD, and so it is hard for them to practice sitting down for a long period of time. Having a structure and group support can be helpful for them so that they don't feel like they are doing it alone. There are several centers that teach mindful meditation. Some centers provide 8-week programs that have weekly training sessions of 2.5 hours each along with at-home practice. They generally begin with seated meditations for 5 minutes every day at home and then work up to fifteen to twenty minutes. They also provide you with the option of practicing longer or replacing seated meditation with mindful walking. As some people who have ADHD tend to be better at learning visually, some centers also use visual aids such as a photo of a cloudy sky in order to describe the principle concepts. The clouds represent all the sensations, feelings, and thoughts that pass by, and the blue sky depicts an area of awareness.

However, your ADHD won't get much better if you do it for just a few minutes a day. Even though the meditation sessions are essential, the key is to be mindful of your actions throughout the day by being aware of where you are focused while you're performing your daily activities. For instance, you might notice that when you are behind the wheel, your attention often goes to the chores you need to do later that day. A majority of people follow mindfulness while eating. You can use the techniques of mindfulness anytime you begin to feel overwhelmed once you are accustomed to checking in with your mind and body.

- **Make it Your Own** – Individuals who have ADHD are encouraged to use mindfulness while performing their daily activities. You can even practice mindfulness on your own. Simply, choose a comfortable place where no one would disturb you and sit down and spend five minutes concentrating on the feelings of breathing in and breathing out. Concentrate on how you feel when your stomach rises and falls. In some time, you will begin to notice that your mind is wandering off to something else – your plans for the day or some noise you just heard or your job. Label these thoughts as "thinking" and put your attention back on your breath.

  Try to perform this mental exercise every day. Increase the duration of time you spend on the mental training every couple of weeks – ten minutes, fifteen, up to twenty minutes, or even more if you want to. Try performing the same exercise every day and concentrate on your breath for some time as you are sitting in front of your computer, or when you are stopped at a red light, or when you are walking from one place to another. By doing this, you can eventually practice mindfulness at any moment, even while you are conversing with others. Turning on your state of mind-awareness any time during the day is a great exercise, even if it is only for a few minutes. You are essentially letting go of the busy-ness of your thoughts and bring your focus back to everything that is happening in the present moment in daily life.

- **Practice Self-Compassion** – People suffering from the challenges of ADHD for several years can be left with crippled self-esteem. You can learn to be more accepting of your weaknesses and strengths through self-compassion. Having an attitude of acceptance can also help improve and manage your areas of weaknesses. For instance, if you are more compassionate towards your problems with time management, then you don't have to pretend that you don't have a problem. You can get proactive about having the tools to manage your time properly without having to feel shameful every time you get late.

Studies examining the non-pharmacological interventions for individuals suffering from ADHD have increased in recent years and given several more treatment options for patients. Current empirical studies back the logic behind using mindfulness techniques to alleviate ADHD. They also provide promising basic-level support for suggesting the usefulness of mindfulness sessions (John T. Mitchell, 2015).

In one study, a mindfulness meditation program conducted in a group was administered to a sample of adolescents and adults with ADHD for eight weeks. Pre- and post-treatment assessments showed that there was an improvement in anxious, depressive, hyperactive-impulsive, and inattentive symptoms.

A study conducted in 2008 with eight adolescents and twenty-five adults, half of whom suffered from the combined type of ADHD (both hyperactive and inactive), revealed that the results were very promising. Significant improvements in both hyperactivity and inattention were observed through the study. The cognitive tests showed that the participants improved their ability to stay focused on one thing even when several other things were competing for their attention. It was also revealed that the majority of them felt less sad and stressed out when the study was completed.

Another study which came out in the *Journal of Child and Family Studies* in the year 2011 studied the outcome of a mindfulness-based training program that took place over the duration of eight weeks (Saskia van der Oord, 2011). The participants included children within the age of eight to twelve years, and a parallel mindful training was also being conducted for their parents. The study reported a significant decrease in the symptoms of ADHD, as were reported by the parents after the eight-week training program. There was also a decrease in over-reactivity and parental stress.

Exercise and ADHD

ADHD can affect both children as well as adults. It can make it difficult for adults to finish their tasks, control their emotions, and pay attention. Similar to children, adults are also given medications and stimulants to control their symptoms of ADHD. They also have therapy sessions that help them stay focused and get organized. Just like mindfulness meditation, exercise is another such method of treatment for ADHD that doesn't require a visit to a therapist's office or a prescription. Studies show that exercising regularly can improve the symptoms of ADHD in adults and also improve their thinking ability.

Studies have shown that exercise is not only good for toning muscles and shedding fat; it can also help you to keep your brain in good shape. Broad science says that exercise can help manage ADHD by increasing the release of neurotransmitters. Chemicals known as neurotransmitters are released by your brain when you exercise. These neurotransmitters include norepinephrine and dopamine, which helps with clear thinking and attention. Individuals suffering from ADHD tend to have a lesser amount of dopamine in their brains. The stimulants and medicines that are used for the treatment of ADHD in adults increase the level of dopamine available to the brain. Therefore, it can be said that a workout session can have similar effects like stimulant medications. Regular exercise can increase the baseline levels of norepinephrine and dopamine by increasing the development of several new receptors in specific regions of the brain.

It also helps to balance the level of norepinephrine in the arousal center located in the stem of the brain. The tone of the locus coeruleus is improved through chronic exercise. As a result of this, people are less prone to react out of proportion or get startled because of any given situation. They also fell less irritable. In the same way, exercise also administers the transmission fluids for the basal ganglia, which causes the smooth changes of the attention system. This region is an essential site for binding the stimulants, and brain scans also reveal that it is not normal in people suffering from ADHD.

Exercising can benefit other regions of the brain as well. For example, an overactive cerebellum can contribute to fidgetiness. According to several recent studies, these regions are brought back into balance by ADHD medications that can increase the levels of norepinephrine and dopamine. And when it comes to increasing the levels of norepinephrine, if the exercise is complex, it gets better.

Some of the benefits that exercise can provide for adults suffering from ADHD are:

- Improve the level of brain-derived neurotrophic factors that are involved in memory and learning. This protein is present in lesser amounts in people suffering from ADHD.

- Improves executive functions that are required to remember details, organize, and plan.

- Improves working memory

- Decreases compulsive behavior and improves impulse control

- Ease anxiety and stress

Any kinds of physical activities like skateboarding, whitewater paddling, mountain biking, rock climbing, gymnastics, ice skating, ballet, and martial arts are very good for adults suffering from ADHD. The technical movements that are used to perform these kinds of physical activities active a huge array of brain regions that help control intense focus and concentration, inhibition, fine motor adjustments, error connection, switching, evaluating consequences, sequencing, timing, and control balance. In the extreme, when you engage in these activities, it also becomes a matter of survival – preventing yourself from drowning in the swirling pool of whitewater, or hurting yourself on the balance beam, or avoiding a karate chop. Thus, it helps you to tap into the concentrating power of your mind's fight-or-flight response. You feel plenty of motivation to learn the techniques that are required for such activities when your mind is on high alert. For the brain, it would feel like a do or die situation. And, thus you will be in the aerobic range while taking part in these activities, which will make it easier for you to learn new strategies and moves and also boost your cognitive abilities.

Exercise also helps regulate the amygdale and has a good effect on the limbic system. In people with ADHD, the amygdale can help blunt the hair-trigger responsiveness that is experienced by several people and sends the reaction to another source of stimulus. This prevents you from going overboard and creating a scene out of anger.

Common Types of Exercises That Help Alleviate the Symptoms of ADHD

For a majority of patients, exercise is recommended as a method to help manage their symptoms of ADHD. Several studies have revealed that one of the best treatments for children and adults with ADHD is regular exercise. This is mainly because exercise helps them get rid of the extra raw energy present in their bodies in a healthy manner. Here are some of the common types of exercises that help alleviate the symptoms of ADHD:

- **Walking** – Walking is one of the simplest aerobic exercises that you can do. What's great about walking is that it can be done by almost anyone of any age group. All you require is a great pair of shoes. The benefits of walking doubles if you walk outdoors. Walking helps tone your leg muscles and also increases your heart rate. Children and adults suffering from ADHD can also benefit from being outside surrounded by greenery. A research conducted on children with ADHD revealed that even walking in the park for twenty minutes can help improve their concentration.

- **Dancing** – Many people suffering from ADHD find dance classes very appealing as a social form of exercise. The best kinds of dances are those that involve fast-paced movements that give you the opportunity to release all your extra energy. A research conducted in Sweden with boys aged five to seven found that participating in dance classes helped them to increase their concentration while doing their schoolwork and also helped to calm them down.

- **Swimming** – Swimming is another aerobic exercise that can help you tone your muscles and improve your heart rate. People suffering from ADHD can get a big boost from being in a swim team because even though they are part of a team, they have to perform individually. It might be hard for people suffering from ADHD to be a part of a sports team if they have to spend a lot of time just waiting for their turn to play. An individual sport like swimming can be a great exercise for this reason.

- **Yoga** – Yoga is extremely deliberate and slow, while people suffering from ADHD are extremely hyperactive. Research has revealed that yoga can be a good form of exercise for you, even if you are suffering from ADHD, because it helps you to focus on yourself. It teaches you to pay attention to your own body and concentrate on your breathing. It forces you to be in the present moment by becoming grounded. Doing yoga can thus help you learn how to concentrate and focus better.

- **Martial arts** – Different forms of martial arts like tai chi, aikido, tae-kwon-do, karate, etc. requires your full attention both mentally and physically. In addition to that, martial arts have a set of fixed rules which need to be followed. This helps add more structure to your everyday life. They can help you feel relaxed and focused at the same time, and this can help you alleviate your symptoms of ADHD. One of the most helpful martial arts is tai chi, as it is also a meditative practice. It can help boost your concentration skills and relieve your stress. Research has revealed that practicing tai chi regularly can help you develop higher levels of self-confidence and focus on other activities. You get trained in several skills like fine motor skills, consequences of actions, memory, timing, balance, focus, and concentration when you do martial arts.

- **Strength training** — You can go for aerobic exercises such as jogging, swimming, and walking first if you are just starting to exercise. You can add in some strength work after you have done simple aerobic exercises for a while in order to add some variety. You can try exercises like weightlifting, pull-ups, pushups, squats, lunges, etc.

Similar to medicines, exercise can also help you alleviate the symptoms of ADHD if you continue doing them. Here are some tips by which you can stay on course if you have difficulty with your attention span:

- **Move in the morning** — Try exercising first thing in the morning if it fits in your schedule. Doing it in the morning before you have taken your medications can help you get the most benefits from all the medications that you are going to take throughout the day to boost your mood. It can also help set the right tone for the rest of the day.

- **Find a partner** — Exercising with a workout buddy can help pass the time and help you stay on track while you sweat.

- **Keep it interesting** — Mix different types of exercises in your routine. If you change your activity every week or every day, it can help you stay out of a rut.

Just like any medications, the effects of exercise can only last for a specific time. Consider your workout routine as a dose of treatment. Try to exercise for thirty to forty minutes at least once a day, for four to five days a week. It is up to you to choose the kind of exercise you want to do but make sure that it is moderately intense so that your muscles feel tired, you sweat, you breathe harder and faster, and your heart rate goes up during the workout session. If you are not sure about how intense your routine should be, you should always consult your doctor. Your doctor might suggest you wear some device like a heart monitor to ensure that you are getting the most out of exercising.

Chapter 4: How Can You Minimize the Triggers?

There are so many things that can trigger your ADHD symptoms. These factors can be either environmental or biological. It differs from person to person. In this chapter, I am going to walk you through the different triggers of ADHD and what steps you can take in order to prevent them from triggering you. As you already know that ADHD is a lifelong problem, it cannot be cured. But you can definitely take steps to make the symptoms bearable, and one such step is to know your triggers and minimize them.

Some Common Triggers to be Aware of

Here is a list of common triggers responsible for making the symptoms of ADHD worse.

Food Additives

There are some parties who believe that symptoms of ADHD can be caused by additives in food, whereas there are some who oppose this view. So, a debate has been going on for quite some time. There was a review that was done in the year 2012 regarding ADHD symptoms and artificial food colorings (L. Eugene Arnold, 2012). In this review, a link was established between the two. It also stated that artificial food coloring is definitely not one of the main causes of ADHD, but it can also be said that the presence of these in food can make a child more prone to be diagnosed with ADHD. But the evidence was inconclusive, and thus, nothing can be said with certainty.

In the same year, another meta-analysis was done, and a very similar conclusion was reached to establish a link between ADHD and artificial food colorings (Joel T. Nigg, 2012). There were a total of twenty-four studies conducted under this analysis, and it said that exposure to artificial food colorings made approximately 8% of kids display ADHD symptoms.

Mineral Deficiencies

Yes, you have heard me right. Mineral deficiencies can, in fact, trigger the symptoms of ADHD. When you are under the treatment process, the medications often have a common side effect, that is, suppressed appetite (Amelia Villagomez, 2014). Stimulants mostly cause this. So, when a person is not hungry, they eat less food, and this causes several deficiencies in the body of the person, including mineral deficiencies. This can make the symptoms spiral out of control.

There are certain minerals whose deficiency in the body can cause symptoms that are very similar to that of ADHD. One such mineral is zinc, and this has been proven by research (Michael H. Bloch, 2014). The symptoms that occur as a result of zinc deficiency are the late development of cognition, restlessness, and inattentiveness.

However, I must say that there has been no conclusive study in this field that could prove that ADHD can be caused by mineral deficiencies. At the same time, levels of zinc being lower than normal has been found in children who have been diagnosed with ADHD. And these studies have also shown that using supplements of zinc during the treatment of ADHD can actually help in managing the symptoms.

Stress

Many people are confused as to whether stress can lead to ADHD in adults. Well, the ADHD episodes can definitely be triggered when you are under a lot of stress. But at the same time, you have to remember that those who have ADHD are often under a continuous state of tension and stress because their life seems to be a mess. So, it often is a vicious cycle. A person with ADHD cannot restrain from reacting severely to nominal situations, and this often leads to elevated stress levels. Other things that can add to this increasing level of stress are procrastinating about important tasks, deadlines that are knocking on the door, and not being able to focus. All of these things make the person anxious, which is, in turn, just the symptom that manifests gives rise to stress.

But we all know that stress is somewhat inevitable in our lives and so what we have to do is that we have to find a middle ground. Both emotional and cognitive challenges have to be addressed. Maintaining proper routines also helps. In Chapter 3, we already saw how mindfulness meditation could be beneficial for

ADHD, and practicing it can also help you alleviate stress.

If stress is left unmanaged, then the symptoms of ADHD can get aggravated. So, make it a practice to evaluate your stress from time to time. Follow techniques that will help you cope with your stress. I will mention some points in the second part of this chapter.

Poor Sleep

Not getting enough sleep is another of the reasons behind the symptoms of ADHD getting aggravated. Now, one of the major medications that are used for treating ADHD are stimulants, and according to the experts, these medications have the ability to cause a rise in the dopamine levels in some parts of the CNS or central nervous system and the brain. This increase in the level of dopamine is what assists in dealing with ADHD, but at the same time, it also increases the possibility of disturbed sleep or no sleep at all.

When stimulants are prescribed, a tendency of not being able to sleep is noticed in patients. In fact, they can also experience daytime sleepiness resulting from waking up from time to time at night. And, when people do not sleep well, they often feel lethargic during the day, and this, in turn, can intensify the symptoms of ADHD. It can lead to impulsivity, indecisiveness, and inattentiveness. Having a good night's sleep is very important for ADHD patients. It has also been noticed that patients often experience sleep problems when the stimulants are administered before bedtime. So, you must talk to your doctor regarding this and fix a time other than bedtime to take your medication.

You cannot afford to compromise on your sleep because it will lead to a lot of problems in your life and hamper your professional life as well. Your ability to comprehend and concentrate will decline. So, it is essential that you sleep for at least seven to eight hours every day.

Technology

There are many controversies regarding whether technology can add to the problem of ADHD and intensify the symptoms or not. It is said that symptoms can be aggravated if a person with ADHD has too much exposure to cell phones, computers, or the internet, in general. As far as watching the television is concerned, there has been confusion, but it is agreed that the symptoms are intensified to some extent. But don't get me wrong – I am not saying that loud music or watching something on the television would lead to ADHD. But if you are someone who is already struggling with increasing your concentration power, then watching television for long is only going to make it worse.

If there is some pent-up energy inside of you that you need to let go, then go and hit the gym or do some physical work. It will help you way more than just sitting in front of the TV. You can also go out with your friends and have some fun. If you are still finding it hard to regulate your time spent in front of the TV, then I would say that you should form a routine where you will have fixed hours throughout the day for everything. This will help you set limited time frames for watching TV or anything that involves you sitting in front of the screen. In fact, there have been several studies that say computer screens, televisions, and mobile phones can cause overstimulation that triggers ADHD symptoms.

Even though there are no specific formal guidelines that tell you the number of hours that can be spent in front of the screen for an ADHD patient, but you can try limiting it after consulting with your doctor.

Tips for Minimizing Triggers

So, now that you know about the common triggers of ADHD symptoms, here are some tips on how you can reduce them.

Maintain a Balanced Diet

Maintaining a balanced diet is very important for not only reducing the triggers but also for preventing ADHD, according to some studies. But what is a balanced diet? Well, a simple definition of a balanced diet is something that includes a well-proportionate amount of all nutrients. So, the foods that you should definitely include in your diet are whole grains, whole fruits, vegetables, different protein sources, healthy fats (oils like olive oil, canola oil, and so on), low-fat dairy, and so on. If you are not aware of where to start then, you can consult a dietician.

If you are taking stimulant medications for ADHD, then you might face symptoms of appetite suppression, and it is quite common. So, you have to make sure that your diet has all the important nutrients; otherwise, you will become deficient in several essential nutrients. If you see that your weight is reducing drastically, then you should consult your doctor because your medication might need to be changed. You might be given an alternate medicine, or your dosage might be adjusted.

Exercise Regularly

I have already emphasized the importance of exercise in Chapter 3. You will also find some common exercises to start with in that chapter. It has been noticed that regular exercise in ADHD patients has helped them improve their cognitive performance to some extent.

Apart from exercise, you should also try mindfulness meditation because it will help you calm your mind and also relieve yourself from stress.

Work On Your Time Management Skills

It is important for every adult suffering from ADHD to brush up on their time management skills. Missing deadlines and procrastinating are very common in patients with ADHD, and this is also what leads to stress. The idea of time is very differently perceived in patients with ADHD as compared to others and so, working on time management skills is so important. It is important that you keep a clock on your desk at all times, which will help you keep track of time. Moreover, take note of the time when you are starting your task and then plant to finish it within a certain time period. For this, you can use timers. Working within a limited time span will prevent the ADHD mind from being scattered and inattentive. The timer will let you know when your limited time is over. If you are doing something that required you to work for an extended period of time, then you can set your timer to go off after regular intervals. After each interval, you can take five-minute breaks. This will help in boosting your productivity. Maintaining a timer like this will also keep you aware of the amount of time that is passing by.

It is also important to make the right estimation of the time that you are going to need. Don't constrict your tasks within a very short span of time. This will put too much stress on you. So, even if you think you are going to need an hour for a task, make sure you keep ten minutes extra on top of the one hour so that you have a time cushion.

In the same way, if you have an appointment at 5 pm, note it down in your calendar at 4:50 pm so that you have ten minutes extra at hand. This will give you time to prepare or have your back even if you are late for some reason. You should set reminders for even the smallest task so that you don't forget anything.

Spend Time Outdoors

Even if you are not exercising or going for a morning run, it is important that you spend some of your time outdoors in nature. Working out is, of course, the best option. But if you don't feel like it on some days, just go to the park and sit on a bench. The sunshine and the fresh air is going to help a lot in reducing stress. Try to spend time somewhere where there is lush greenery. If you live in a city, go to a park. The greenery is soothing to the eyes and has a feel-good vibe.

Get Enough Sleep

Like I told you before, ADHD symptoms can get triggered when you are not getting proper sleep. So, if you want to stay attentive during the day and work productively, then you need to sleep properly at night. The first thing that you need to do is not having caffeine in the second half of the day. Exercising regularly also helps in having a good sleep but make sure you don't exercise just before going to bed. Your sleeping cycle has to be maintained even on weekends. Maintain a fixed time not only for waking up in the morning but also for going to bed at night. This will bring you into a fixed routine and will help your body adjust to its sleep-wake cycle. Create your own bedtime routine that is not too elaborate and yet gives you peace. It can be taking a soothing bath and then using some relaxing skin products. You can listen to a particular soothing playlist or whatever makes you feel relaxed.

For some people, drinking a cup of warm tea is helpful. But you should select the right tea as well. Chamomile tea is really great for sleep. Whatever tea you choose, you need to make sure that there is no caffeine content in it. Make your dinner light. If your dinner is too heavy, you are more likely to feel bloated. This causes discomfort and hampers sleep. So, you can even have a light snack.

Before going to bed, you need to prepare your brain for sleep. So, you can practice some quiet time. This means that you have to practice relaxation and not listen to anything loud or watch TV. You can even practice reading a bit if that is something you love to do. You can play sounds of ocean waves or crickets because they are highly relaxing.

Some ADHD patients have also said that aromatherapy has helped them a lot in terms of sleeping. So, you can try oils like chamomile, jasmine, and lavender because all of them are well known for promoting good sleep.

Try to think about happy things before going to bed. Steer clear of all those negative thoughts because they are not going to help you in any way. Practicing positive thinking is really a good habit to release stress and prevent anxiety during bedtime.

You need to avoid all those things that can hamper your sleep. This also includes sugary foods. When you eat or drinks sugary items, it automatically gives your body an energy boost, which is also known as the sugar rush. It keeps you awake and is, thus, not ideal before bedtime.

While you can practice these strategies on your own, if you think that you are being triggered frequently, it is best that you consult with your doctor.

Chapter 5: Behavioral Therapy for ADHD

It is the medication that helps an ADHD patient on the neurological level, but in order to make day-to-day life easier, therapy is extremely important. Behavioral therapy is a basic or preliminary therapeutic approach that an ADHD patient is exposed to. The therapy starts in their childhood years. In adulthood, the therapy changes into CBT or Cognitive Behavioral Therapy. Before moving into the details of CBT, I would like to briefly discuss with you the behavioral therapy in kids.

How Does Behavioral Therapy Work?

When we talk about going to therapy, what we picture in our minds is a therapist talking to his/her patient. But that is not how every type of therapy looks like. In fact, behavioral therapy is quite different. Here, the emotions of the person are not the main focus – the focus is on the actions and how they can be rectified.

When a child or an adult is taken to a therapist, the therapist will first understand the state of the problem and then prepare a plan with the help of which you can work towards solving your problem. The main idea is to get rid of all the toxic and negative habits and simultaneously, replacing those bad things with positive habits. In the case of kids, behavioral therapy does not only involve the kids but also the parents.

This is because the parents are the ones responsible for the upbringing of the child – they have a great influence on the mind of the child. There are so many parents of ADHD kids who get frustrated and start yelling at the kid even though the kid did not do it on purpose. So, a major part of behavioral therapy is also about making parents understand their kids and change their own behaviors towards the kids.

No matter what the type of behavioral therapy is, a system of rewards and consequences is always set up. The rewards have to be chosen very carefully. The rewards have to be something that motivates the patient and makes him/her truly work hard towards achieving their goals.

There are a lot of ways in which behavioral therapy can be helpful. In the case of kids, it helps them in keeping their anger in check and then slowly helps themselves get adjusted to social settings. They learn how they should perceive each situation and then react in a reasonable manner. They learn various tactics of self-control. Since the main aim is to inculcate good habits in the child, the rewards that are chosen for the therapy should also reinforce good behavior in the patient.

But when you notice that rewards are not really helpful, then you have to take a different approach. That is when the concept of consequences, particularly negative consequences, walks in. If the patient does not do something as asked, then he/she will lose points – this is what negative consequences look like.

CBT for Adults

There have several research and clinical results that support the fact that adults with ADHD can benefit a lot from CBT or cognitive behavioral therapy. The patient is not only happier, but they also show higher levels of happiness, are highly productive, and their self-esteem also gets a boost. Here, in this section, I am going to tell you more about CBT and how it helps ADHD patients.

What Is CBT?

Cognitive behavioral therapy or CBT is primarily a talking therapy, and it is done over the short-term to bring a change in the way people think and instill healthy thought patterns. Adults with ADHD have already undergone a lifetime of poor self-esteem, continually missing deadlines, and forgetfulness. But this goal-oriented therapy that mostly involves concepts of psychotherapy can help the patient change his/her thoughts about the world, their own self, and their future. All the negative thoughts are replaced with positive ones. In short, CBT can be termed as specialized training for the brain.

The main idea behind CBT is to bring a change in how the person perceives the events of their lives. It also deals with how they behave in such situations. Both these things ultimately have an immense effect on how the person feels. Whether a person is dealing with complicated relationships, stress, or negativity, CBT can help in every aspect. In fact, studies have proven the usefulness of CBT. The quality of life of the patient can be significantly improved by introducing CBT. This therapy is not only used in the case of ADHD patients but for a whole range of other problems as well. These include drug use problems, alcohol problems, anxiety problems, and also depression. It has also been noticed that compared to other forms of psychiatric medications, CBT can give better results.

The main principles on which the idea of CBT is based are as follows –

- It is considered that partly, every psychological problem is somehow a result of unhelpful or faulty thinking patterns.

- It is also considered that partly, every psychological problem is a result of unhelpful or learned behavioral patterns.

- Better coping methods can be learned by patients with a psychological problem, which would help them manage their symptoms and lead a better life.

So, if we have to put in words, CBT is not only a goal-oriented treatment method but also one that is very specific to the problem at hand. It addresses the behaviors and thoughts of the patient and all the challenges they are facing in the present day. CBT can be done in both group and one-on-one therapy sessions. So, honestly, it is quite a broad concept, and the treatment can be designed to focus on specific aspects of your life. But both the counselor and the patient will have to collaborate together in order to make it work. There will be a series of sessions.

Initially, CBT was mainly used for people suffering from mood disorders. After that, it branched out to other problems. All of us have automatic thoughts as a reaction to different situations. But these thoughts are the reason why we face so many problems in our emotional state. CBT addresses these thoughts and helps you correct your spontaneous interpretation of things. Our spontaneous interpretations are not always correct, and the main reason behind this is that they are biased and influenced by different types of distortions. These internal dialogs are so ingrained in our minds that they act as an obstruction in making the right decision. So, whenever you are trying to calculate the risk or do something productive, your mental distortions will hinder you.

But once you start CBT, you will notice what a significant impact it can have on your life. Completing tasks and staying on a particular task for an extended period will become easier with CBT because the problematic thought patterns will be changed. All the distorted cognitions that you have will be challenged by CBT, and thus, your behavioral patterns will change.

How Does CBT Help ADHD Adults?

Now, let us see how CBT works to give you a better life. As you already know, the self-regulation skills of people are gravely affected through ADHD. The direct result of this is that the executive functioning skills of the adult are affected. It is also why ADHD adults suffer from emotional dysregulation, disastrous time management skills, inconsistent motivation, disorganization, procrastination, and impulsivity. But all these problems that I have mentioned here are not yet included in the different criteria for diagnosing ADHD even though the patients display these symptoms.

It is often seen that adults who have been diagnosed with ADHD have a pessimistic attitude towards life. They become highly self-critical. The main reason behind all of this is that there are several setbacks that they have to endure both in everyday life and social settings. When situations don't go as planned (which is often the case), ADHD patients spiral into a cycle of self-blame. But what is worse is that these patients start projecting their pessimistic thoughts onto their future as well. Just because they had a bad day, they think that every other day that is going to come will be bad as well.

ADHD patients can't seem the logic in things because their thought processes are entirely clouded by their demoralizing beliefs and thoughts. It also hinders their possibility of growth and being productive.

Here, I am going to list of the distorted thinking patterns that adults with ADHD experience. CBT helps in correcting all these patterns —

- **All-or-nothing thinking** — This type of thinking pattern is when a person consistently uses words like ever or never (i.e., absolute words). This thinking pattern is very common in people irrespective of whether they have ADHD or not. When someone indulges in this type of thinking, they can only think in extremes. No matter how much they try, they cannot seem to get out of the black-and-white terms. What they have to do is understand that there are a lot of gray areas in life. This faulty thinking pattern also makes people overlook any alternative solutions that might be present. And in the case of ADHD patients, this type of thinking promotes them to think only about the downside of things. Thus, these patients either see themselves as a complete failure, or they think they are highly successful. If they make a small mistake in their project, they immediately start discrediting all of the efforts they have put into the project and start thinking that they have failed.

- **Mind reading** — This cognitive distortion is when a person automatically assumes that they know what the person in front of them is thinking. This distortion is very dangerous because people fail to notice what is right in front of them just because they are too engrossed in their idea of things. They rely so much on their self-proclaimed ability to read minds that they sometimes end up misreading others' intentions. It leads to sudden bouts of frustration and anxiety. The direct result of mind reading is social anxiety, and in the case of ADHD patients, this is even more magnified because ADHD adults already suffer from a certain extent of social anxiety.

- **Overgeneralization** – Overgeneralization is when people make some pretty broad assumptions about things even when their experience in that matter is limited. There are different forms in which overgeneralization can manifest itself. But it mostly revolves around the fact that once a person notices something negative, they start thinking everything is going to be negative. In short, they allow one singular event to predict every outcome that is to follow. For example, just because you didn't get the job after giving an interview, you start thinking you are not going to get any of them because you are not good enough. This thought process brings about a feeling of hopelessness.

- **Fortune-telling** – This is another type of cognitive distortion seen in ADHD patients where they claim that they know the future, and it is going to be bad. The roots of this type of thought pattern are based on anxiety. But there is a difference between making an educated guess and fortune-telling. When you are predicting things simply on the basis of assumptions, that is when you are fortune-telling as a part of your cognitive distortion. Thus, the real odds are never considered, and so you cannot call fortune telling a real form of assessment. For example, if your job interview went bad, you can probably assess it, but there is no way of knowing for sure whether or not you are going to get the job. There might be a hundred reasons why you will get the job. You don't know how your competitors performed or whether their personality is a good fit for the job. So, if you still assume that you are not going to get the job despite the fact that you don't know a lot of factors, then you are fortune-telling.

- **Personalization** – This is another type of cognitive distortion that ADHD adults go through. In this type of negative thought pattern, the person keeps blaming themselves for everything that happened wrong. Or, the person blames someone else. No matter who the person is blaming, the situation was totally out of control, and in reality, no one is at fault. For example, when ADHD patients cannot perform well in a professional career, they blame themselves that only if they had put in some more effort, there would have been no complications. But things are not like that –

ADHD is a problem whose symptoms will hamper your everyday life, and you have no control over that.

- **Comparative thinking** – This type of thinking is what brings inferiority complexes and makes us feel that we cannot achieve things. Sometimes, the comparisons made are not even realistic, and yet people continue to believe them. ADHD patients have been commonly found to give in to comparative thinking. Every person on earth has his/her own weaknesses and strengths, and so comparisons are not something that you should do.

- **Mental filtering** – This is a specific type of faulty thought pattern that is found not only in people with ADHD but also in others. When a person has the habit of mental filtering, he/she filters out all the good and positive things and directs all their focus on the negative things. Thus, in simpler terms, people with mental filtering are the ones who always find their glass half empty. They are so focused on their dissatisfaction and inadequacies that they miss out on all the fun. Their feels are often rooted in loneliness. The only way to overcome this particular cognitive distortion is to focus on reframing your negative thoughts.

- **Emotional reasoning** – Lastly, this is another type of cognitive distortion commonly seen in ADHD patients where they think that their reality is reflected by their negative feelings. So, let us say that you are tensed, and so you think you are in danger – this is what emotional reasoning looks like. This often leads to exaggerations of problems that are too insignificant.

When you go for CBT, your therapist will help you understand your thoughts, and you will also learn to identify the different types of cognitive distortions on your own. When you widen your perception of a situation, your reaction is also expanded into something that is less defensive. With CBT, you will learn to address your fears and your insecurities slowly but steadily. There will be plenty of activities through which the therapist will ease you into the process. There will be role-playing activities and also assignments given to you as a part of your homework.

With time, you will notice that you no longer jump to conclusions like before, or you don't give in to a negative mindset as your default setting. One very common problem among patients of ADHD is procrastination. Keeping track of time seems to be a major issue, but not everyone suffers in the same way. For each patient, the therapist will ask him/her to describe a recent situation where procrastination got the better of them. After listening to the incident, a specific goal for that patient will be set. The goal can be something as commonplace as shopping groceries.

The relationship of the patient with that of the task is analyzed because this will help the therapist chalk out the plan that you are going to follow. After that, the task will be broken down into simple, actionable steps. Each step is then analyzed to find out whether any potential barriers might arise and if yes, then what steps can be followed to overcome those barriers. While doing all of this, the therapist will also ask the patient about what they are thinking during each step. They will also you what emotions are crossing your mind and how do you feel when you are finally facing the task that you had been putting off for so long.

I am not saying that the process is going to be easy because it won't. There will be a lot of obstacles that you will have to cross in order to be successful. But what is invaluable is the fact that you will be discussing your ADHD problems at length with a professional, and this itself is going to be so refreshing and helpful. In fact, some patients also say that the mere act of discussion is so therapeutic.

You should also keep in mind that in order to get success through CBT, you also need to go to an expert. Also, since CBT is used for a variety of psychological problems, there are several CBT therapists who are not aware of how to treat ADHD. So, whoever you got to just make sure you have asked them about their experience of handling ADHD patients. The ADHD specialty clinics are now growing in number with each passing day, and you can also contact these clinics to know about any qualified therapists near you who can help you with CBT. So, if an orderly life is what you want, don't waste any more time and look for a CBT specialist today.

Another thing for which you will get help from CBT is the comorbid conditions. Hypersensitivity often leads to anxiety, and CBT helps address all the issues and comorbid conditions of ADHD. Every condition is treated with a different approach in the case of CBT.

What Is DBT?

Next up, we are going to discuss another type of therapy option that is available for ADHD adults, and it is known as Dialectical Behavioral Therapy. It is quite similar to CBT because this one is also focused on mitigating the challenges faced by a patient on an emotional and social level.

Initially, it was only the patients of BPD or borderline personality who were treated with DBT, but now, it is being used in several problems. The therapy mainly focuses on teaching emotional regulation skills, and in the case of ADHD patients, these skills prove to be very fruitful in leading an everyday life.

Chapter 6: A Step-by-Step Guide to Become More Productive With ADHD

Adults with ADHD often go through days when they feel like they cannot do anything. They cannot think straight, nor can they stay focused on any task—this inability to focus hampers their productivity levels. But the worst part is that this feeling is very often what every day looks like for an ADHD patient. We all know that when it comes to productivity, the most common rules that apply to usual circumstances are prioritize, focus, and delegate. However, these rules cannot be used in the case of an ADHD patient. It is because the ADHD brain works differently.

But no matter how many obstacles stand in your path, it doesn't mean that you cannot be productive. You can definitely learn some strategies that will help you manage your time and stay up to date with work. So, in this chapter, we are going to have a look at some of the most common productivity tips that are extremely useful for ADHD patients and will help you handle every distraction that comes your way.

Step 1 - Don't Try Multitasking

People often think that multitasking is the answer to your problems but trust me, it is not. Multitasking will only complicate things further for an ADHD patient.

If you want to get something done, the first and foremost thing is that you need to stay focused. So, for a person who is easily distracted, doing one thing at a time is a big challenge. If that person were to do multiple things at a time, think how hard it is going to be for him/her to stay focused. Every task on that person's list ends up staying incomplete.

You might think that multitasking is going to save time, but it is quite the opposite. When you have to do many things at once, the ADHD brain is not able to work efficiently. The main reason behind this is that there is a constant shift of focus from one task to another, so the brain basically keeps doing back and forth. Every time the brain has to focus on something new, it takes a couple of seconds to readjust. Even if it doesn't seem much to you, these seconds keep adding up, and at the end of the day, multitasking is the reason why you are left with incomplete tasks.

But the problem is, multitasking has become like second nature to most of us. Here are some things that you can do to avoid multitasking –

- Firstly, you have to find out the pairs of activities that you usually tend to multitask. Then, sort them into groups. All tasks that have some kind of familiarity between them can be sorted together in one group. For example, you can watch TV and file your nails at the same time. But you definitely should not answer your emails while watching TV. The idea is to separate the daily tasks which can be grouped together to multitask and save time. But the more complex tasks should be set aside.

- For the tasks that you have pointed out as complex, you need to block time in your planner. This time span will be solely devoted to completing that one single task. When you are spending time doing that one single task, you need to keep your phone away. You can also put up a board on your door that says 'do not disturb.' If you think that the new project that has been assigned to you is not the typical easy ones and you need extra time to complete it, then let your client know about it.

- Try developing a morning routine. A morning routine might not be directly related to multitasking, but it helps you establish a pattern, and you will do the same things every day in the same order. Moreover, a routine will increase your familiarity with a single task, and the more you do it, the more familiar you will find it. And then, after a certain point of time, that task might become so familiar to you that you can add it to your list of tasks that are multitaskable.

Lastly, I would like to say, no matter what, you should try not to multitask because it has been seen that the more people try to multitask, the more they are late at completing things. This makes them work on the weekends or stay up late every night just to catch up with everything. The result of all this is stress, and you definitely don't want more of that in your life.

Step 2 - Be Realistic

Being realistic is one of the major things to learn in order to increase your productivity with ADHD. You have to understand that since you have ADHD, your brain is not like that of others. It is different, and the concept of time is also different.

So, when you decide a time frame for your tasks, you need to be quite realistic about it. Keep in mind that every task is going to take much longer than you think it would. So, plan some extra time in your schedules so that you don't have to run at the last minute to cover your deadline. Also, whenever you are planning your tasks and your time frames, include small breaks in between. This will prevent your brain from getting tired, and you will stay energized throughout. Taking breaks in between is all the more important for patients with ADHD; otherwise, your concentration levels will falter.

Thus, you simply have to follow the rule of 'under-promise and over-deliver.' Make it your motto. If you are an optimistic and career-oriented person, you already have an idea in your mind regarding the number of things you can do in a day. But when you promise people around you that you are going to deliver the service within a time period and then fail to deliver it, there is no value in your promise. Moreover, this will also create a constant pressure upon you. So, the trick is to commit less and deliver more. This will not only enhance the satisfaction of the clients but also improve your productivity levels and give you more motivation.

Step 3 – Stop Trying to be Perfect

The need to be perfect at all times is often the biggest hindrance that we have on our paths. And for an ADHD patient, this is all the more true. You have to understand that sometimes it is okay to make mistakes and not do things perfectly. In order to be productive, sometimes you have to allow your laundry to keep stacking in the corner of the room and order takeout. You need to learn to cut yourself some slack from time to time because you are not a machine. Perfectionism is your enemy, and you cannot give in to it. The more you chase perfectionism, the more you will ask yourself whether you are enough. The truth is – 'You are enough.' It doesn't require you to be perfect to be enough. Being perfect is an illusion, and you have to break free.

If you think that you want to be perfect, then you will constantly be chasing something or the other in your life – be it more beauty, wealth, more promotions, or anything. The road of being perfect is always dissatisfying because it will drive you down a track where you will keep wanting for more, and there is no end to that.

Don't depend on others to make you feel worthy because that is also how perfectionism keeps growing. You will never feel enough if you keep relying on others. It is a deceptive cycle. External validation will inevitably make you feel that you need more to feel enough. So, you need to bring a change to your mindset. Set expectations that are realistic and always put your well-being first. Your perception of the world depends quite largely on how you see it. People are not born with the idea of self-reliance. You have to learn it. The moment you do that, you will realize that you are in more control of the situation than you thought you were. It will not only boost your happiness but also your sense of self-esteem. Accept yourself for the person you are.

Stop telling yourself that you are a failure. This type of negative self-talk is not going to get you anywhere in life. It will not convince you to accept yourself. What you need to do is make yourself believe that you are good just the way you are.

One of the most prominent aspects of striving to be perfect is the need to always get it right. The moment things go a bit off-road, people feel like a failure. But you have to make yourself understand that the fact that you are trying to achieve your goal and putting yourself out there is a huge accomplishment. So, make progress and give a pat on your back because you deserve it.

Step 4 – Prep Your Environment

The next thing to do if you want to be productive is to prep your environment. It will elevate productivity levels by helping you to focus. Whether you are working from home or from your office, your environment plays a significant role in your productivity.

Here are some things that you should keep in mind –

- **Lighting** – The first aspect to take care of is the lighting. If you want to feel inspired to work and churn out more ideas, you'd be amazed to know what a great role lighting plays in it. But even then, people often overlook this factor. You will feel irritated and put a lot of strain on your eyes when your workspace doesn't have sufficient lighting. In fact, it has been found that people become depressed when they work in dark spaces. If you are working from your cubicle at the office and the general lighting is not enough, don't be shy to bring your own light. But if you are working from home, things are in your control. So, allow as much natural light as you can. Open all the windows. If the day is cloudy, make sure you switch on the lights.

- **Table and chair** – Now, let us talk about the type of chair and table that you should use. When your table and chair are not of the right type, you will often find yourself moving or stretching from time to time. For the best ergonomics, your feet should not be dangling. They should be either resting on the floor or on a footrest. Your eye level should match with that of the top of the monitor. The distance between your eyes and the computer screen should be at least 24-36 inches. In order to avoid or prevent any kind of back pain, the chair posture needs to be a bit reclined. But if you are working in a company, you can't do anything about the chair. What you can do is add some pillows to adjust your back. But if you are having a height problem with the chair, you can ask for a riser. Investing in a good-quality chair is what you should do if you are working from your home.

- **Reduce clutter** – ADHD patients often forget to clean their spaces, but clutter will only hamper your productivity, and you cannot afford to do that. In your office, you obviously do not have control over the clutter generated in the whole area. But you can definitely keep your own workspace clean. Make it a routine to clean your desk every evening before you leave, and every morning when you come. Just set everything in place and start your day fresh. It will help minimize the distraction. When you are working from home, the chances of clutter increase a lot. Everything that is in your house can distract you. If you are someone who stays busy most of the time, then you will need to have a professional cleaner to help you out. But if you want to save money, then you have to fix a day in a week when you will clean everything. Apart from this, set aside fifteen minutes of your time every day to clean your home office.

- **Room temperature** – You might be surprised to know that room temperature does play a role in your productivity. It applies even more to ADHD patients because they tend to get irritated by the slightest things. Your productivity increases with warmer rooms. But in offices, the general temperature that is maintained is 65-68 F, and this is not the ideal range for productivity. Since you cannot control the temperature of your office, you can bring a space heater for your cabin. But if you are at home, you need to adjust the temperature depending on the weather.

- **Room scents** – Your mood is hugely affected by the different scents in your surroundings, and so you should do something about it. If you feel that you have been drifting off quite frequently, then keeping some aromatic substances in your surroundings might help you focus. For example, the smell of cinnamon can help you maintain your focus for longer periods, the smell of citrus helps in lifting up your mood and keeps you awake, the smell of lavender should be used after a long and tiring day at work to help you relax, and the smell of pine keeps you alert. Remember that if you are working in an area where you have others close to you, then you should use scents that are subtle and won't disturb others. But if you are at home, then you can use essential oils or candles.

- **Level of noise** – The level of noise is something that is very often not in our hands to control. The company culture and the size of your team are some of the things affecting the noise. The design of your office also plays a role. But we cannot deny the fact that our concentration levels depend on the noise to a huge extent. If the levels are way above average, then you might find it difficult to concentrate, and your productivity will take a hit. While working from home, people often think that maintaining a quiet space can be attention boosting, but it is quite the opposite. Complete silence is often a distraction in itself. So, you can play some mild sounds that boost your concentration. White noise is a very good example. If you are working from your office or a place that is too noisy, always carry your noise-canceling headphones. They can be a real savior in such situations.

Step 5 – Time Your Tasks

In this step, we are going to learn how you can time your tasks and how beneficial it is when it comes to time management. Timing your tasks can actually give you a better sense of time. And it is also quite simple to do. All you need is to set the alarm on your phone or use a timer. ADHD patients often struggle with procrastination. Timing the tasks will help you deal with it effectively. Fix a particular amount of time for a particular task and then start working. But whatever time you choose, make sure you are not pushing yourself too much. You will know that it is time to start the next task when your timer goes off.

Similarly, when ADHD patients start doing something that they love, they tend to spend the entire day on the task. In order to prevent that, timing the task will let you know that you have already spent a specific amount of time on that task, and now, it is time to move on. It is advisable that you use a timer for every task that you do in the day, be it running errands for home or working on projects at your office.

Timing your tasks will also help you keep track of all those areas where you are less productive, and then, you can work on these areas separately. Every activity that is present on your to-do list for the day should be assigned a specific time span.

Step 6 – Do the Fun Stuff First

I know that many of you believe in doing the difficult things first so that by the time half the day has passed, you are done with the tricky tasks. But in the case of ADHD patients, if the day starts with tasks that pose a lot of resistance, it is easier for them to lose focus. So, it is advised that you do the easier things first. Or, you can start with the things you love doing.

Moreover, when you finish the good things first, it will not take you much time. The sense of accomplishment that you will get on completing those tasks will motivate you to work more and get more things done.

Taking small steps at the beginning of the day will prevent you from getting overwhelmed.

Step 7 – Use Visual Reminders

Visual reminders have often proved to be very helpful for ADHD patients to remember stuff. Moreover, you can be as creative as you want while planning these visual reminders. Decorate your office walls with boards where you can put up your deadlines and personal acronyms to remind you of the tasks that you need to get done. You can also put up rules that you need to follow.

Make sure you put up these reminders and deadlines where it is easy for you to notice them. It will also constantly remind you to use your time productively. You can also take the help of sticky notes to put up reminders on your desk, on your computer screen, or wherever you feel would be easier to notice. You can also set productive screensavers on your computer so that even when you are taking a break, you always have a quote boosting you up.

So, I hope that you follow all these steps mentions here, but the most important thing to keep in mind is that our own negative self-talk is what holds us back. No matter how many tips you follow, if you don't stop automatic negation in your mind, it is only going to put you in a counterproductive path.

Chapter 7: Treating ADHD With Medication

Is it okay to use medications for ADHD? Do these medications have any side effects? I understand that you might have several such questions in your mind, and in this chapter, we are going to address all those issues.

It is true that the symptoms of ADHD can be kept in control with the help of medication. This applies to both adults and children. You can get a hold on impulsivity, inattentiveness, and hyperactivity by taking the right medications. But you also have to understand that there are several risks and side effects associated with these medications. Moreover, if you have gone through Chapter 5, then you already know that medications are not the only form of treatment option available to you. Whether you are an ADHD patient yourself or a family member, it is of utmost importance that you have all the knowledge about ADHD medications. Having a comprehensive knowledge will help you make the right decisions and go with the best options.

Before going into too many details, one of the most basic things to understand is how these medications can help an ADHD patient and what their limitations are. For starters, taking the right medications will help the patient stay focused on the task at hand, plan things properly, and get a grip on their impulses. But you also have to remember that medications cannot do any magic. You will notice that the patient is suffering from certain symptoms like social anxiety and forgetfulness from time to time, even when they are taking the medications. So, a lot of other changes in the daily lifestyle of the patient is also required for any long-term change. This includes maintaining a proper sleep cycle, following a healthy diet, and doing some regular exercise.

Remember that no matter what medication you use, ADHD is a lifelong problem, and it will not be cured by medication. But when you take the meds, you will get relief from the nagging symptoms. Some patients think that now that they are not having symptoms, they can stop the meds. But the moment they do that, the symptoms come back, and they are worse. Another thing to keep in mind is that the medications don't work equally on everyone. If someone you know is benefitting a lot from a certain medication, it is not that you will get the same level of benefits. You might only notice some modest development while the other person might witness dramatic changes. The reaction of a patient to a particular ADHD medication is quite unpredictable. The main reason behind this is that every person has a different response to the medication.

That is why when you visit a doctor, he/she will diagnose you, examine the intensity and type of your symptoms, and then prescribe you a dosage that is solely meant for you. The medications are extremely personalized. Even after that, you should visit the doctor for regular check-ups. ADHD might go out of hand and become a risk if you do not visit the doctor from time to time. The medications need to be monitored very closely.

Stimulant Medications

There are basically two groups of medications that are used in the treatment process of this disorder. One of them is the stimulant medications. They mostly help you by controlling hyperactivity, reigning in impulsive behavior, and stretching the short attention span of the patient. Sometimes, patients are treated solely with the help of stimulant medication, and at other times, some kind of therapy is used along with the meds.

It has been found that about 70-80% of the children and 70% of the adults with ADHD have seen an improvement in their symptoms once they started using stimulant medications. The meds have also proved to be fruitful in helping patients to improve their relationships. If the patients keep on taking the medications without fail, then they witness not only better behavioral tendencies but also a much more focused life. However, there is still not enough evidence supporting the fact that medications can help in regulating the social life of patients.

Another interesting fact to keep in mind about the stimulant medications is that they have been in use for the longest time when it comes to ADHD treatment. Their effectiveness in this field is backed up several studies. Some familiar names in this group of medications are Dexedrine, Adderall, and Ritalin.

The main working mechanism of stimulant drugs is that they help in increasing the levels of dopamine in the brain. Now, for your knowledge, there are several neurotransmitters in the brain, and dopamine is just one of them. It is mainly responsible for movement, attention, pleasure, and motivation. Most ADHD patients have reported that they have received significant benefits after taking stimulant medications in terms of improved focus and concentration levels.

Now, there are two types of stimulant medications that are used. They are as follows –

- **Long-acting stimulants** – These medications are usually prescribed to be taken only once in a day. It is because their effect lingers for a long time period, usually for about eight to twelve hours. They are also known as extended-release stimulants. These medications are also more commonly preferred. When people have ADHD, they have trouble remembering stuff, and so, if they have to take medications multiple times in a day, it becomes difficult. But in the case of long-acting stimulants, they only need to take the meds once a day. Thus, it is a much more convenient option.

- **Short-acting stimulants** — The other type of stimulant medications are the short-acting ones. As the name suggests, the effect of these meds is very short-lived, and their peak effect is felt after several hours of consumption. They need to be taken at least two times a day and sometimes even three.

Now, let us talk about some of the common side effects that stimulant medications have –

- Upset stomach
- Dizziness
- Frequent mood swings and irritability
- Feeling jittery and restless
- Tics
- Sleeping irregularities
- Headache
- Fast-paced heartbeat
- Increase in blood pressure
- Reduced appetite
- Depression
- Nervousness

Apart from the ones that are mentioned above, some patients also notice changes in their personality after taking stimulant medications. Some people have reported becoming more talkative, whereas others become rigid or listless. There have also been cases where patients became less spontaneous and somewhat withdrawn from life.

There are certain side effects that do not linger for long. These include upset stomach and headache. They might go away once the patient becomes accustomed to the medication. Your body will take time to adjust itself to this new medication, but once that time period is over, you should get better. But you will have to inform your doctor if the side effects remain for a longer time.

For side effects that don't go away on their own, a change in medication is usually required. In some cases, people are allergic to certain stimulant medications. The allergy might manifest itself in the form of a rash or skin pigmentation. Keep an eye out for such signs, and if you notice anything of that sort, you have to inform your doctor at once.

Now that we have discussed the different side effects of these medications, it is time you are made known about other safety concerns that are associated with taking stimulant medications.

- **Heart** – Let us first see what effect these medications have on your heart. When adults with pre-existing heart conditions take these stimulant medications over the long-term, sudden death has been noticed in some of these patients. That is why it is advised by experts before you start any type of stimulant medication for ADHD, you should definitely get a cardiac evaluation done. And, if the person already has a history of problems related to the cardiovascular system, then an electrocardiogram should be done.

- **Developing brain** – When stimulant medications are administered to kids with ADHD or adolescents, the effect on the developing brain has not yet been clearly determined. But it is a common fear among the researchers that brain development might be hampered when children are exposed to stimulant medications over the long-term.

- **Substance abuse** – It is a very growing concern among the families of ADHD patients because stimulant medications often lead to substance abuse problems. This is even more common in young adults and teens. The fact that stimulant medications can cause a loss in weight has also added to this problem. So, if someone in your house is taking the stimulant medication, you have to be aware as to whether they are selling these or sharing them with someone else.

- **Psychiatric problems** – Some psychiatric problems are triggered by the use of stimulant medications. These problems include paranoia, depression, anxiety, aggression, and hostility. If the ADHD patient already has a family history of bipolar disorder, depression, or suicide, then they are more at risk of developing these problems. So, when a patient is taking stimulant medications, they should miss an appointment with their doctor because these medications have to be closely monitored at all times.

Here is a list of people who are advised against taking stimulant medications –

- Patients who have been diagnosed with a coronary artery disease

- Patients who have hyperthyroidism

- Patients who already have past instances of drug abuse

- Patients who suffer from problems where their heartbeat is not normal and is irregular

- Patients who have glaucoma

- Patients who have been found to be allergic to stimulant medications

- Patients who suffer from frequent bouts of anxiety

- Patients who have had psychotic episodes in the past
- Patients with tics

If you are still confused about when you should call your doctor, then here are some red flags that you should be aware of –

- Fainting
- Difficulty in breathing
- Pain in the chest
- Paranoia or suspicion
- Having auditory or visual hallucinations

If you notice any of the above-mentioned signs in the patient, you need to call the doctor at once.

Non-Stimulant Medications

In the previous section, we talked about stimulant mediations, but they are not the only type of drugs used to control ADHD symptoms. There is another type of drug known as non-stimulant drugs. These include several medications used for controlling blood pressure, antidepressants, and also Strattera. Usually, doctors don't prescribe non-stimulant medications right away. The first choice is always the stimulant medication. But if the patient cannot be prescribed stimulant medication due to some existing health problems or the stimulant medications are not working for him/her, then the non-stimulant medications are prescribed.

So, let us talk about these non-stimulant medications one by one.

Strattera. This non-stimulant is used for ADHD treatment quite commonly, and it has also been approved by the FDA. The medicines are also popularly known by its generic name – which is – atomoxetine. In the previous section, I told you how the dopamine levels in the brain are affected by stimulant medications. In the case of Strattera, it is the levels of norepinephrine that is increased.

When compared to the other types of non-stimulant medications, it is found that the effect of Strattera on the human body is quite long-lived. In fact, you can get relief from the symptoms for an entire day. Thus, for people who find it challenging to get up in the morning, this medication is quite a good option. Another positive point about Strattera is that it helps in curbing depression. So, if a patient is already suffering from depression and anxiety along with ADHD, then Strattera is a very good choice of medication for them. Moreover, it doesn't matter whether the patient has Tourette's Syndrome or tics; they can still have this medication. Aside from all this, the effectiveness of Strattera in treating the symptoms of ADHD are comparable to that of stimulant medications.

Some of the commonly seen side effects in patients using Strattera are as follows – frequent mood swings, vomiting or nausea, upset stomach, pain in the abdomen, dizziness, headache, and feeling lethargic or sleepy. Some uncommon side effects of Strattera are reduced appetite and difficulty in sleeping.

Now, let us move on to some other types of non-stimulants that are used in the treatment of ADHD. But these are not approved by the FDA and are 'off-label.' These medications are not usually prescribed by doctors until and unless Straterra doesn't seem to be working. The first category of medicines is antidepressants.

Antidepressants. These medications are usually preferred for those patients who are not only suffering from ADHD but also have symptoms of depression. The antidepressants that are prescribed to the patients in these cases aim at more than one neurotransmitter—the most popularly used antidepressant, in this case, Wellbutrin. Bupropion is the generic name of this medicine. This medicine aims at both dopamine and norepinephrine. Apart from this, there is another line of treatment open to the doctors, which involves the use of tricyclic antidepressants. The side effects of this medication are quite mild, but the patient might experience a loss of appetite, irritability, worsening, or Tourette's syndrome or tics, and decreased sleep.

Medications for high blood pressure. These medications are also used in the treatment of ADHD. But not all medications of this category are suitable for ADHD treatment. Some common names include guanfacine or Tenex and clonidine or Catapres. However, it has been reported that these medications do not help with increasing attention. But they are helpful in decreasing hyperactivity, aggression, and impulsivity.

When Should I Take Medications?

This is the most common question that is asked by the ADHD patients. Even though it might seem like an easy decision, it is not. Today, people are aware of a lot of facts regarding ADHD, and yet they are not enough to make this decision. Well, what I can tell you is that you shouldn't make this decision in a hurry. Think it through and take your time if you are still unsure. Judge all the options that are present in front of you. But lastly, you should never overlook your instinct. If you get a gut feeling that this is going to be good for you, go with it. If your doctor is telling you to take the medication, consider it but never let anyone pressurize you into taking certain types of meds.

If you want to have a better idea about the medications in ADHD treatment, then you should visit a specialist and clarify your queries. Some common things that you should ask are as follows –

- Is medication absolutely necessary to help me manage my symptoms?

- What are the treatment options that I have in front of me?

- What is the effectiveness of these medications?

- Considering my symptoms, what is your choice of medications for me? Do these medications have any side effects?

- During the course of the treatment, will the medications have to be taken throughout?

- How will I know when I have to stop taking the medications? What are the signs?

Remember that taking medications is not the only type of treatment approach there is for ADHD. The challenges posed by ADHD can be conquered by other methods as well, and the patient can still lead a life that is productive. Here, I am listing some common strategies that have to be used alongside the medications so that your dosage can be kept low.

- For starters, what you eat is very important. Your diet should be healthy. Your diet not only has a direct effect on your symptoms, but it can also uplift your mood and help you concentrate. If you eat the right type of food, you will find yourself with greater energy levels than before. So, have a fixed time for eating your meals and also include some snacks in your meal plan in between the major meals. Your diet should be rich in magnesium, iron, and zinc alongside the omega-3 fatty acids.

- The next thing to do is to have a regular exercise schedule. Exercising daily doesn't mean that you have to do some kind of intense workout. Any type of physical activity helps elevate the levels of serotonin, norepinephrine, and dopamine. Your ability to stay attentive and focused is affected by all of these neurochemicals. If you don't want to hit the gym, you can also try dancing, skateboarding, or simply walking. Do anything you love that involves burning some calories. Put down your mobile phone on weekends and go outside for a walk. You will automatically feel replenished.

- Give a shot at therapy. Coping with your problems can become easier with therapy. In Chapter 5, I have already explained the different types of therapy, the approaches used, and their benefits. In ADHD, there are certain habits of the patient that can flare up the symptoms, but therapy can solve this problem. There are certain therapies that are mainly focused on teaching you impulse control, and there are others that teach you how to reduce stress. You will also learn how to organize your life and manage your time. All of this will ultimately help you in achieving your goals.

- Having a good sleep at night is equally important, like everything else mentioned above. Once you start sleeping well, you will notice how drastically your symptoms are improving. Sleeping well at night is not that difficult. All you need to do is make some small changes in your sleeping habits and you will be noticing some really good changes. For starters, don't drink caffeine in the second half of the day. Also, try to set a fixed time for going to bed at night.

- Lastly, staying positive can make a massive difference in the result of the treatment. If you stay happy and positive minded, nothing can pull you down, and you will get better results.

I would also like to remind you that if you decide to start taking the medications as prescribed by your doctor, you also have to promise yourself that you are going to maintain the schedule. In order to get the effectiveness of the medications, following instructions is of utmost importance. You need to know everything about those medications, and your doctor is the best person to ask.

Also, you might not find the right medication for you in the first try. It's like a hit-and-trial method. So, you have to communicate openly and be honest in order to find the medication that suits you best.

Chapter 8: Dealing With ADHD Shame

Shame is something that lots of adult ADHD patients feel, and it can be deafening. The root cause of shame lies mostly in the fact that ADHD patients feel they have not been able to keep up others' expectations and have been a complete failure throughout their life. If not addressed, the sense of failure can hamper self-esteem and become a very big emotional burden. So, you should never be afraid to go to someone and ask them for help, especially professional help. If you are feeling sorry and perpetually unworthy, then you are also a victim of ADHD shame. It can be a haunting thing to endure for a lifetime. That is why it is of utmost importance that you find out the root cause of your shame, understand why you have to do something about it, and then take the necessary steps.

What Is Shame?

Even though it might seem unrealistic, people do misunderstand the concept of shame and mix it up with other feelings. In order to prevent, first, you must have a comprehensive idea of what shame is. If you are someone struggling with ADHD, then you already know that every day feels like you keep apologizing to others for something or the other. It might be because you didn't do the laundry, didn't clean your desk, were late to the office, or lost your car keys. No matter how hard the ADHD patients try, these things keep happening over and over again.

It eventually leads to a cycle of self-blame where apologizing for even insignificant things, becomes a habit. It happens even more in those patients who were diagnosed with ADHD later in life. Ultimately, these patients are numbed by the sense of shame, and it can be very crippling. Things can go to such an extent where people refrain from looking into their wardrobe because they know it's messy, and they are ashamed of it. They feel tortured for every disorganized part of their lives.

So, to put it in simpler terms, shame can be described as a constant state of embarrassment and feeling of inadequacy. The person feels as if he/she is humiliated all the time. In extreme cases, people are no longer the person they really are in front of others, and this gives them a feeling of having a secret life. Out of all the symptoms that ADHD patients have to face, shame is definitely one of the most painful ones, and it can easily wreak emotional havoc. The patients keep indulging in negative self-talk, and it is more or less like wearing an anvil throughout your life.

Thus, when people experience shame, they are somehow ashamed of a certain part of themselves. They struggle a lot in their daily life, but they don't want others to know about it. So, they put up a façade where they lead a happy life. But with time, this constant need to be someone else brings a feeling of loneliness, and it is exhausting. The patients start withdrawing themselves from their close ones as well, and eventually, they can't seek support from their family members because they are crippled by shame.

There are different types of shame in ADHD, and we are going to discuss them below –

- The first type of shame is where the person is simply ashamed of the fact that they have ADHD. They cannot be comfortable with this medical condition. Even though it is a lifelong condition and people have to accept it as if they have different hair colors, it is not so easy.

- The next type of shame that ADHD patients feel is that they are different from others. They look at others, and then they look at themselves. They notice significant differences. This shame of not being the same as others is more crippling in children than in adults. Everyone has the desire to fit in, but with ADHD, you will always have differences that will make you stand out in the room (and not in a good way). This constant attention that ADHD patients receive when they walk into a room also gives them social anxiety. But it is not only the behavioral differences that set them apart, ADHD patients often need extra help, and they also have to take meds throughout the day and keep up with their doctor's appointments.

- The next type of shame that ADHD patients have is about their behaviors. They do not behave the same as others. They almost always end up doing something where others make them feel embarrassed. They feel embarrassed because their work desk or their home is not as tidy and clean as that of others'. Every person is affected differently when it comes to behavioral shame. But all of them have one thing in common – they are ashamed.

- Another common type of shame noticed in ADHD adults is that they are not satisfied with their position in life, and they feel that they did not put in enough effort. They had set certain goals, and they feel like they haven't reached those milestones. The shame from this feeling is worsened when they see others around them doing great things while they can't. This also causes resentment because the ADHD adults are just as smart as the others, and yet they have drawbacks.

- ADHD patients keep ruminating about their pasts, and they bring up every instance in their minds where they failed at doing something. It can be the time they missed paying their credit card bill or the time when they had to break up with someone special. It can also be the most embarrassing moment of their life. They keep playing it over and over again, and they relive that shame from time to time.

You should also understand that shame and guilt are two very different things. You feel guilty about what you have done but you feel ashamed of who you are as a person.

Consequences of Shame

Now that you have a clear idea of what shame is let us move on to the consequences of ADHD shame. As you already know, people with ADHD face intense emotions. Whatever normal emotions they have are intensified to a great extent. And, shame can lead to some pretty nasty emotions. Here are some of the common ways in which shame can affect the lives of ADHD patients –

- People try to conceal their own personalities because they feel ashamed. They avoid any situation where they have to be emotionally vulnerable, and this impacts their relationships to a great extent. We are going to explore how ADHD impacts relationships in greater detail in the next chapter. But for now, you should know that ADHD patients shy away from friendships or even intimacy because revealing their personality and who they are, makes them feel vulnerable.

- ADHD shame makes the patients not express their emotions. They start bottling up a lot of feelings. This leads to depression. The tendency to suppress one's emotions is even more common in women as compared to men. They might be ashamed of an incident that happened to them, or they might be ashamed of the person they are. Whatever the reason is, the person keeps suppressing all his emotions and thoughts inside their heart, and this eventually leads to severe mental health conditions.

- The direct result of both the above-mentioned consequences is that the ADHD patient is pushed into a state of constant anxiety, depression, and worthlessness. Their self-esteem takes a hit and becomes impaired. Every day in their life feels like a battle that they have to endure.

- Relapse into more severe phases is more common in those ADHD patients who face shame in a more intense manner. Someone who might have overcome substance abuse might relapse back into it just because they have this crippling sense of shame at the back of their heads. In fact, there have been cases where people purposefully gave into problematic behavior just because they think healing is not possible for them. That is why it is said by specialists that very often, the reason why ADHD patients don't consider therapy or any form of treatment is because of the shame they have. They think that since they are worthless, there is no point in opting for treatment.

So, as you can see from the points mentioned above, shame pushes you into a cycle of self-rumination and negative self-talk. Sometimes people try to cease that pain by turning to alcohol or drugs, both of which make the problem worse. In extreme cases, shame takes the shape of anger, and people start becoming aggressive. Even when their loved ones try to help them out, they push everyone away. If you are a family member of an ADHD patient reading this book, then I would urge you to understand that when the patient is pushing you away, that is when they need you the most. They simply don't see it, and so, you cannot give up on them.

How to Silence the Haters?

One of the main sources of ADHD shame is the haters in the society who don't know anything about the disorder and yet, treat it as an untouchable thing. The reason behind this is the several misconceptions that are present in society. But if you want to deal with ADHD shame and not let it control you, then you have to silence the skeptics, and we are going to talk about it in this section.

Very often, you will find that skeptics make it absolutely clear that adults cannot have ADHD and that they are simply using it as an excuse to cover up their faults. They keep saying that whatever symptoms they are having or claim to have is because their parents did not hold the reins when they were young. They will tell you to deal with your shortcomings and grow up. But I have already given you plenty of evidence in this book to support the fact that ADHD is real. It is very real, and it happens in adults as well. So, if you do have to reply to the skeptics, do so with facts. One of the best ammunition you can produce in front of the skeptics of society is a hard fact. You can even take him/her to one of your meetings with your support group or send them articles that will educate them.

But if you are looking for something sarcastic, you can always tell them how nice it is for them to be smarter than some of the most renowned psychologists and scientists in the world.

Then comes another group of people who are best described as the crusaders. They will question every step you take and every decision you make. They will second guess your choice of doctor or even your medication. They might even tell you that ADHD medications are nothing but 'kiddie cocaine,' but then, you have to present them with facts that, like every other medication, ADHD meds have their side-effects too. But that does not mean they are going to inculcate a feeling of dependency in the patient. Before you go spouting off things to others, you need to make sure you have your facts straight. So, read as many articles as you can so that you can make an informed speech about how drug therapy is actually important for ADHD patients.

At the end of the day, you have to let go of others think of you. You need to focus on yourself and your decisions. Ask yourself – do you want to take medications? Do medications make you feel better? Are you comfortable with taking medications? If the answer to these questions is yes, then who cares what others think? So, the next time someone comes to you with their holier than thou attitude about drug therapy, you can simply ask them would they deny taking insulin if they had been diagnosed with diabetes?

Then there are some people who like to make sarcastic jokes about ADHD symptoms. They might say things like 'If only I had ADHD, I could come up with some excuse for forgetting deadlines every month.' When you protest, saying that these comments are disrespectful, they might say they were simply joking. The best way to deal with such people is to ignore them and not respond until the right moment comes. For example, if it is your boss who keeps humiliating you for your ADHD, you should avoid responding to those comments. Start looking for a new job, and when you find one, you can write a detailed report to the main office stating how your boss abused you just because of a medical condition. If you think you cannot put up with it any longer, you can use the direct approach and see how your boss responds. You can tell them that these comments are hurtful, and you'd like him not to continue being sarcastic. If this works, then it is okay; if it doesn't, then you have to wait for the right time to submit a written complaint.

The next type of people are the ones closest to us and yet fail to understand that ADHD is a real problem. No matter how much evidence you provide them, they will not believe you. They might keep telling you that there is nothing wrong with you, and you are simply being lazy. Experts believe that family members often behave in such a manner because of the fact that they cannot accept that anything like ADHD exists. Moreover, they cannot accept that it might run in their family, so they go into denial. So, if you have someone like that in your family, you have to stand up to them and let them know that ADHD is a condition that you are suffering from, and it is not about them. In the beginning, it might be difficult, but as time passes, these types of people will give up.

How to Heal Shame?

No matter how you reply to the haters of the society, the shame lingers on, and you have to figure out a way to heal yourself. No matter how much qualified a person becomes in life if they feel ashamed because of ADHD, no degree or educational qualification can reduce it. Eliminating shame is something that is not possible for everyone. There is some amount of shame in all of us but what you can do is reduce the toxic levels of shame, and here are some tips on how you can do it –

- **Educate yourself** – The first step is to obviously educate yourself about ADHD so that you don't have any misconceptions. Understand that all the behaviors and traits that you have are because of some genetic and neurobiological reasons. It is not about your character, and so there is nothing wrong with you. It is not your fault, and you have to understand that. Different areas of life are hampered because of ADHD, and you are not the only one here. It happens to every patient. Go back to the first two chapters of this book and remind yourself that ADHD is a biological condition. When you educate yourself more and more, it will become easier for you to acknowledge th fact that ADHD is, in fact, a neurological condition. You will realize that many of the causes of your shame are nothing but a result of your ADHD. With time, you will see how the majority of shame was self-inflicted.

- **Have your own support system** – If you don't have people supporting you in your journey to fight ADHD, then you need to build one right now. It can be a local support group where you go for meetings, meet similar people, and share your experiences. Or, it can also be your therapist or any family member who truly understand you and supports you. When you connect with people who understand the problem, you will feel heard. If you have a busy lifestyle and you think that you cannot make time for support groups in your locality, you can also search for online support groups. Some of them even conduct webinars from time to time.

- **Change your mindset** – Pay careful attention to how you think of yourself or how you talk to people when you have to talk about yourself. Do you talk too much in negatives? Do you say things like 'I am never going to become good at managing time'? If yes, then it is time you change these things. You should say that 'I know it is difficult, but I can slowly learn how to manage my time'. Such sentences promote hope and motivation. Several people think that bringing a shift in your mindset is about neglecting the problem. But that is not the case – you have to change yourself to a positive person where you are open to all possibilities. You will let go of your limiting beliefs. You will stop judging yourself and start believing that it is okay to make mistakes but what is important is that you are ready to fix them.

Practice Self-Love

Loving yourself can be really helpful in overcoming ADHD shame. You may find it strange and difficult in the beginning because you are used to blaming yourself for every small thing and being ashamed of who you are. Put yourself first and look out for your happiness and well-being. This will surely help you to heal from shame. Let us discuss some of the self-love practices that you can do to become a fully functioning and self-sufficient individual who can take care of themselves and live a happy life.

Take Help From Others
If you love yourself, never hesitate to ask for help and to receive help. We are social creatures, and we constantly need each other to survive. When you are overwhelmed, anxious, confused, or lonely, make sure that you reach out to people instead of sinking in your own grief and shame. Sometimes a good company can provide you guidance and comfort. If you let your grief and emotions get the best of you, then you will not be able to calm yourself or think. People think that asking for help is what weak people do, but it is not like that. If you help others at their difficult times, then you deserve to get helped in your crisis as well. When your problems are serious and persistent, go to your friends, family, or someone professional like a therapist.

Meet Your Own Needs
Pay attention to yourself and cater to your needs. If you keep on worrying about meeting the needs of others and neglect your own needs and concerns, then you will end up nowhere. It is high time that you stop all these things and start putting yourself first. In case you are habituated with someone else taking care of all your needs, then you need to stop that as well.

With ADHD, it can be difficult, but doing some things on your own will make you feel better. Make sure that you meet the basic physical needs like a dental checkup, medical checkup, exercise, rest, food, etc. Give a little extra attention to those needs and requirements which you are most likely to overlook. When you feel tired, confused, overwhelmed, afraid, angry, sad, lonely, or victimized, try asking yourself what will comfort you and go for it straight away. The reason for your depression may also be the fact that you have been neglecting and avoiding yourself for a prolonged time.

Start Having Fun
Start planning hobbies, recreation, and pleasures. If you keep on focusing on the gloomy side of your life and constantly stay overwhelmed with your problems, your life will become a competition or a struggle of achievement and endurance. Life should not be a burden, so don't go too hard on yourself. Sometimes, a little bit of enjoyment and laughter is all you need to get back on track.

Protect Yourself
Protecting yourself from mental, emotional, and physical abuse is an essential part of self-love. If you love someone, then that doesn't mean that you have to accept mean and insulting behaviors from them. If you think that you are abused or violated, stop wasting your energy and time in expecting to change that person. Take a stand for yourself and cut them off your life. In the section 'How to Silence the Haters?' I

have explained some of the ways you can stand up for yourself. But if situations arise that are not mentioned, be creative and deal with the haters with a stern hand. Never blame yourself for the hate spewed upon you by others.

Be Gentle to Yourself
Treat yourself with compassion and gentleness. Make your inner voice a little kind and calm towards yourself. When you are in pain or any kind of crisis, blaming yourself will not do any good. It will just make things harder and worse for you. And when you have ADHD, these feelings manifest themselves more intensely. In situations like these, you may be tempted to distract yourself and ignore your feelings, but make sure that you don't do that. Instead, just try to be with yourself. You are the one who should be with yourself the most when you are in fear, anger, hopelessness, sorrow, or anxiety. The innocent child inside of you needs you the most. Try to comfort yourself with compassion, kindness, and tenderness, just the way you do for others. Listen to yourself and start forgiving yourself. Embrace yourself and build trust in yourself. Never give up on yourself.

Start Accepting Yourself
Loving and accepting yourself includes your shortcomings, thoughts, feelings, and appearance. You don't need to prove anything to anybody. You deserve respect and love, regardless of all your flaws. Others will always try to search for opportunities to violate your flaws and weaknesses. Stop seeking

validation from others and accept your own flaws and weaknesses. In this way, you can prevent yourself from getting violated by others and become a spontaneous and authentic person.

Encourage Yourself
Treat yourself with enthusiasm and encouragement. There should be a positive coach inside you who will always encourage you to do things you love. Don't wait for others to give you compliments or appreciation. Give credit for what you are good at, instead of taking those for granted. Encourage yourself to make even the slightest progress towards your dreams and aspirations.

Express Yourself
Don't keep your inner self hidden for too long. Start honoring yourself and communicate your needs, thoughts, opinions, and feelings. Always remember that you have a right to have an opinion that is different from others. You are unique, and you can feel and state whatever you want without owing a justification to anybody. If you start stating your opinions fearlessly, you will start earning other's respect as well. Don't worry about the fact that you have ADHD. Does having diabetes mean that you won't voice your thoughts? No, right? The same goes for ADHD.

Start Having a Spiritual Practice
Start to spend more time with yourself. Regardless of your belief in God, spiritual practice will really help

you to create a deep relationship with yourself. Having some quiet time for your self is a great way of honoring yourself. Religious beliefs are not necessarily required for spiritual practice. By doing this, you can find a place that is calm and centered from where you can access inner guidance for experiencing harmony with others and yourself. When you invest more time in listening to yourself and in finding the truth for yourself, you get peace, clarity, and confidence. It will help you to keep your calm and your mind in the right state no matter what happens around you. In Chapter 3, we have elaborated on the concept of mindfulness meditation.

Lastly, I would like to say that you should go to a therapist who is experienced in working with ADHD patients struggling with shame. Learn to be compassionate because you deserve that. Treat your body in a positive light and yourself as a child. Take care of yourself as a child, and you will see what an incredible difference it can have on your body and mind. You can even prepare a checklist of all things (big and small) that you can do to decrease your sense of shame. The more you let shame take hold of you, the more you will give in to the lies of the society. Have faith in yourself. The path might not be easy, but you have it in yourself to walk upon it.

Chapter 9: ADHD and Relationships

In this chapter, we are solely going to focus on how the different relationships in our lives are affected by ADHD. It is true that it can lead to resentments, frustrations, and several misunderstandings. You will even push away the people who are closest to you. But on the brighter side, there different strategies that you can follow to mend these relationships and lead a happy life.

What Is the Impact of ADHD on Relationships?

The usual symptoms of impulsivity and hypersensitivity can wreak havoc in different areas of your life, but they can also cause a dent in your personal relationships. It can become worse for those who have not yet been diagnosed with ADHD or are not receiving proper treatment.

First, let us see what impact ADHD has on your life if you are the one suffering from ADHD.

- As you might already know, one of the most common symptoms of ADHD is being distracted at all times. But when it comes to relationships, being distracted can cause a lot of problems. Your partner might think that you are neglecting them. Staying distracted at all times might also lead you to not keep up on important promises that you have made. Gradually, your partner will start feeling unwanted and unheard. You might love your partner way too much, but because of the symptoms of ADHD, if you don't show your love for your partner, he/she will start feeling like they have been left alone.

- The next thing that I want to mention is being hyperfocused. This is a tendency noticed in ADHD patients. Sometimes they become so hyperfocused at something that they forget everything in their surroundings. It is somewhat exactly opposite to what distractibility is. Your loved one might start feeling left out or unimportant because you can't seem to drag yourself away from the thing that you are hyperfocused on.

- Next, let's talk about forgetfulness and how it impacts relationships. I don't think I have to emphasize much on how partners might feel if you forget important dates or a dinner date that you were supposed to attend after your meeting. Your husband might feel that you left him stranded just for nothing. You might forget your share of the responsibilities from time to time, like cleaning the house, paying the bills, and so on. Eventually, your partner will feel like they cannot rely on you for even such basic tasks, let alone anything important. In this way, resentment keeps building on both sides.

- We all know that ADHD patients struggle with being organized. They might leave their tasks without finishing them or keep piles of stuff lying here and there. This can be a problem if you are in a relationship with someone who prefers things to be kept tidy and clean. So, you being disorganized is not only stressful for you but also for them. And so, this is what gives birth to constant nagging in relationships with an ADHD person.

- Another very prominent trait of ADHD people is their impulsivity. This can be problematic in relationships. Impulsiveness will prompt you to act before thinking anything through. One very common example of this problem is when you keep spending money without any reason and just because you felt like it. This often results in credit cards being maxed out and too many things in the house, causing a shortage of space. However, there are some ADHD patients who show some more dangerous symptoms of impulsivity – they love to drive recklessly or love to have risky sex. They might even prefer using inappropriate words in public places. All of these things lead to compatibility issues among partners.

- Procrastination in ADHD patients can also affect relationships. For example, whenever you are on tight deadlines because you procrastinated all along, you might be extra fussy and irritated at your partner without proper reason. No one likes to be treated that way, and so this is another reason for disputes in close relationships with ADHD patients.

- Lastly, ADHD patients have terrible mood swings from time to time. At one moment, they are happy, and the next moment, they are terribly angry at some incident, which is insignificant. This leads to frustration and anxiety, both of which can take away the happiness of your relationships. Your partner might constantly feel on edge and this is not good if you want your relationship to be stable.

Now, if you are the person who is in a relationship with someone having ADHD, you will constantly feel that you are unappreciated, ignored, and lonely. You will find your partner not keeping any of the promises they made or not remembering things you wanted them to remember. In fact, you might even feel that the person you love so much doesn't even care about the relationship.

So, now that you have seen how both parties in a relationship are affected, you can understand how destructive it is. But you can fix it and get out of this toxic cycle. Read on to find out how.

Tips for a Healthier Relationship

If you want to turn your relationship into a healthier one, then here are some tips that you should follow –

- **Walk in your partner's shoes** – The first step to mending a broken relationship is to understand your partner. You have to place yourself in their position and then understand their perspective of things. But you also have to keep in mind that it is extremely easy to misunderstand and misinterpret things. If you have ADHD and your partner doesn't, then you have to understand that there are a lot of differences between you both and how you think. So, if you truly want to understand your partner, it's best if you go and ask them.

- **Learn about ADHD** – In order to mend your relationship, you have to know everything there is to know about ADHD. You will understand its influence on you and your partner once you know about the symptoms and why they happen. If your partner doesn't have ADHD, but you are the one who has it, then it is all the more important for your partner to learn about this disorder. Then, it will become easier for him/her to understand your actions.

- **Acknowledge that you need to work on your relationship** – Many a time, relationships falter because the partners fail to notice or rather don't want to acknowledge that their relationship needs work. Constant criticism and nagging are not going to get you anywhere. If you cannot figure out a way yourself, then you should seek professional help and opt for a couple's counseling from a specialist who has experience in dealing with ADHD patients.

- **Take responsibility** – Being responsible for your actions is very important not only for the partner who has ADHD but also for the one who doesn't. You can make progress in your relationship only when you own up to your actions. It is true that the symptoms of ADHD itself cause a lot of problems, but it is not right to put all the blame on the disorder alone. The partner is also at fault. No matter what your symptoms are, it is in your hands how you choose to react to a particular situation. It is your reaction that will determine whether your partner feels loved or ignored.

Now, there are some things I would like to say to the non-ADHD partner because even you have certain responsibilities to take care of. You have to understand what your partner is going through. ADHD can make a person feel constantly guilty and ashamed, and stressed. They are overwhelmed by the simplest things in life. So, if you notice that your partner is experiencing some strong emotions, ask them to take a time out, and then you can talk it through after a while. Acknowledge the fact that it is not always your partner's fault. They are not always unreasonable. Sometimes it is their symptoms acting up. Care for your partner just the way you want them to care for you. Finally, look for ways in which the symptoms of your partner can be managed because once that happens, your relationship will start getting better as well.

Conclusion

Thank you for making it through to the end of *ADHD Workbook for Adults*; let us hope that you were able to get answers to all the questions you had in mind. I hope you have gained some knowledge from the insight that I shared in this book. Each and every strategy that has been mentioned in this book has been proven to bring the symptoms of ADHD under control and make your life easier.

The next step is to apply these strategies in your life so that you can lead a more fulfilled life with your loved ones. I understand that it is not always easy to deal with the symptoms of ADHD every day. It takes a lot of courage to tackle your issues head-on and put in all the hard work that is required to overcome the problems. It is quite probable that the first medicate you take, or the first therapy you seek might not work for you. But don't let that one moment discourage you from the path of seeking treatment because the right treatment is out there; you simply have to find it. There might be several instances where you have to try medications that are not the right fit for you, but only after you try things you will come to know what works for you and what doesn't. I had personally known so many people who had had to try several therapies and medications before they finally got 'the one' they had been looking for. The idea is to never lose hope.

Every journey has its own setbacks, and yours is no different. But there is no need to beat yourself up for a couple of failures. You need to keep reminding yourself to stay strong. Love yourself and give yourself a pat on the back whenever you make the least progress. Tell yourself that every challenge that comes on your path is just another opportunity for you to grow as a human being and learn new things along the way.

The one advice that I give to everyone is that if you want success in your battle against ADHD, you first have to learn how to accept yourself. No matter how many failures you receive, you have to stay excited and motivated for the new opportunities to come. Whenever you are starting to walk on a new path, it is always better that you start with a note of positivity. A positive mind will take you places. Just because you have ADHD doesn't mean that you cannot have a balanced life. You simply have to learn how you can work together with other people and improve your communication skills. If things seem too much to handle on your own, learn to delegate because it is always better to take help from others than do a task all by yourself and ruin it.

You will notice that organization is not your strongest skill set, but you have to come up with something practical that you can follow in your life. Take help from your close people or your family members whom you trust. Think about how you can come up with a system of planning things that will be easier to memorize and not much of a hassle. The moment you come up with a routine, your life will seem less chaotic because now, you have a set of tasks to complete within certain time frames. You should even plan your sleep and your meals so that you don't forget anything.

Agreeing to do too many things at a time can cause a lot of trouble in your life. But your tendency to become impulsive will force you to indulge in such behaviors. That is why it is important for every ADHD patient to learn to say no. The more work you take, the more jam-packed your routine is going to become, leaving you stresses and overwhelmed. Your ability to lead a lifestyle that is healthy depends largely on how well you prioritize your work and other commitments. So, whenever someone presents you with a new opportunity, take a moment to check your schedule and see how much you already have on your plate.

Don't pay heed to any of the ADHD myths or rumors in your surroundings. If you want to know something about ADHD, always read articles from trustworthy pages. Don't let anyone make you feel that you are lazy or using ADHD as an excuse. ADHD is a very real problem, and it is a disorder. Choose your therapist wisely because he/she is going to help you a lot in managing your symptoms.

There are so many challenges that ADHD patients have to face in their day-to-day life. From organizational difficulties to problems in time management, they have to put in more effort than others even when they are doing the simplest tasks. ADHD patients who already have a challenging job to handle find it even more difficult because it is no easy task. But take it one step at a time. Don't try to change everything all at once because that will only leave you even more overwhelmed. No matter what you do, don't overlook the stress that you are taking upon yourself. Keep a check on the stress levels. Engage in some physical activity even if it means going for a stroll in the neighborhood and eat a healthy diet. Practicing these healthy habits will also benefit you in the long-term by reducing your symptoms. Slowly, you will see how manageable your life becomes. Lastly, I would also encourage you to practice mindfulness and yoga, both of which will help in calming your mind. It will also help you exercise greater control over yourself and your emotions. If you are just a beginner, meditate for a shorter time span, and then you can gradually increase it.

I hope that the treatment options and the tips that I had mentioned in this book have come of help to you. If you doubt that you have been suffering from this disorder, then you should not be wasting any more time and meet the doctor at once. The longer you take to seek professional help, the more your condition will deteriorate. The right treatment is out there in front of you, and all you need to do is ask for it.

Finally, I would highly appreciate it if you can leave a review on Amazon if this book has helped you in any manner.

Resources

Alexander T. Vazsonyi, J. M. (2017). It's time: A meta-analysis on the self-control-deviance link. *Journal of Criminal Justice, 48*, 48-63.

Amelia Villagomez, U. R. (2014). Iron, Magnesium, Vitamin D, and Zinc Deficiencies in Children Presenting with Symptoms of Attention-Deficit/Hyperactivity Disorder. *Children, 1*(3), 261-279.

Anne Halmøy, O. B. (2009). Occupational Outcome in Adult ADHD: Impact of Symptom Profile, Comorbid Psychiatric Problems, and Treatment. *Journal of Attention Disorders, 13*(2), 175-187.

Aparajita B. Kuriyan, W. E. (2012). Young Adult Educational and Vocational Outcomes of Children Diagnosed with ADHD. *Journal of Abnormal Child Psychology, 41*(1), 27-41.

Benjamín Piñeiro-Dieguez, V. B.-M.-G.-L. (2016). Psychiatric Comorbidity at the Time of Diagnosis in Adults With ADHD. *Journal of Attention Disorders, 20*(12), 1066-1075.

Joel T. Nigg, K. L. (2012). Meta-Analysis of Attention-Deficit/Hyperactivity Disorder or Attention-Deficit/Hyperactivity Disorder Symptoms, Restriction Diet, and Synthetic Food Color Additives. *Journal of the American Academy of Child & Adolescent Psychiatry, 51*(1), 86-97.

John T. Mitchell, L. Z. (2015). Mindfulness Meditation Training for Attention-

Deficit/Hyperactivity Disorder in Adulthood: Current Empirical Support, Treatment Overview, and Future Directions. *Cognitive and Behavioral Practice, 22*(2), 172-191.

L. Eugene Arnold, N. L. (2012). Artificial Food Colors and Attention-Deficit/Hyperactivity Symptoms: Conclusions to Dye for. *Neurotherapeutics, 9*(3), 599-609.

Michael H. Bloch, J. M. (2014). Nutritional Supplements for the Treatment of ADHD. *Child and Adolescent Psychiatric Clinics of North America, 23*(4), 883-897.

Rucklidge, J. J. (2010). Gender Differences in Attention-Deficit/Hyperactivity Disorder. *Psychiatric Clinics of North America, 33*(2), 357-373.

Saskia van der Oord, S. M. (2011). The Effectiveness of Mindfulness Training for Children with ADHD and Mindful Parenting for their Parents. *Journal of Child and Family Studies, 21*(1), 139-147.

Stéphanie Baggio, A. F. (2018). Prevalence of Attention Deficit Hyperactivity Disorder in Detention Settings: A Systematic Review and Meta-Analysis. *Frontiers in Psychiatry, 9*.

Stephen P. Hinshaw, E. B.-N. (2012). Prospective follow-up of girls with attention-deficit/hyperactivity disorder into early adulthood: Continuing impairment includes elevated risk for suicide attempts and self-injury. *Journal of Consulting and Clinical Psychology, 80*(6), 1041-1051.

Winston Chung, S.-F. J. (2019). Trends in the Prevalence and Incidence of Attention-Deficit/Hyperactivity Disorder Among Adults and Children of Different Racial and Ethnic Groups. *JAMA Network Open, 2*(11).

Ylva Ginsberg, J. Q. (2014). Underdiagnosis of Attention-Deficit/Hyperactivity Disorder in Adult Patients. *The Primary Care Companion For CNS Disorders.*

Zheng Chang, P. D. (2017). Association Between Medication Use for Attention-Deficit/Hyperactivity Disorder and Risk of Motor Vehicle Crashes. *JAMA Psychiatry, 74*(6), 597.

Printed in Great Britain
by Amazon